# PUMPED

Previous publication by these authors also available
in Norton paperback

*Buzzed:*
*The Straight Facts about the Most Used and Abused*
*Drugs from Alcohol to Ecstasy*

# P U M P E D

STRAIGHT FACTS FOR
ATHLETES ABOUT DRUGS,
SUPPLEMENTS, AND TRAINING

*Cynthia Kuhn, Ph.D., Scott Swartzwelder, Ph.D.,*
*and Wilkie Wilson, Ph.D.*

*W. W. Norton & Company  New York  London*

Photos 1, 13, 15–17, 20–24: Copyright Medical Economics Company, *Physicians' Desk Reference*, 1999 edition. Photos 2–12, 18–19, 25–32: Courtesy of the Drug Enforcement Agency, United States Department of Justice, *Drugs of Abuse*, 1997 edition. Photo 14: Courtesy of Dr. Albert Cramm, director of plastic surgery at the University of Iowa (www.surgery.uiowa.edu/surgery/plastic/gyneco.html).

For information about permission to reproduce selections from this book, write to Permissions, W. W. Norton & Company, Inc., 500 Fifth Avenue, New York, NY 10110

The text of this book is composed in Weiss
with the display set in Bank Gothic Medium
Composition by Gina Webster
Manufacturing by Courier Companies, Inc.
Book design by Chris Welch

Libarary of Congress Cataloging-in-Publication Data

Kuhn, Cynthia.
Pumped : straight facts for athletes about drugs, supplements, and training / by Cynthia Kuhn, Scott Swartzwelder, and Wilkie Wilson.
p.      cm.
Includes bibliographical references and index.
ISBN 0-393-32129-0 (pbk.)
1. Doping in sports. 2. Athletes—Drug use. 3. Dietary supplements. I. Swartzwelder, Scott. II. Wilson, Wilkie. III. Title.

RC1230.K8452000
617.1'027–dc21                          00-030455

W. W. Norton & Company, Inc., 500 Fifth Avenue, New York, N.Y. 10110
www.wwnorton.com

W. W. Norton & Company Ltd., 10 Coptic Street, London WC1A 1PU

1 2 3 4 5 6 7 8 9 0

TO OUR FAMILIES

# CONTENTS

*Introduction* 13

*Chapter 1* OPTIMIZING PERFORMANCE 15

*Chapter 2* HOW TO READ THE ADS 30

*Chapter 3* WARMING UP: DRUG BASICS 39

*Chapter 4* BULKING UP/SLIMMING DOWN 50
Diuretics • Appetite Suppressants • "Fat-Burning" Drugs •
"Fat-Blocking" Drugs

*Chapter 5* BUILDING MUSCLE MASS AND STRENGTH 66
Anabolic Steroids • "Natural" Steroids? • Growth
Hormone and Its Friends: IGF (Somatomedin), GHB •
Clenbuterol • Creatine Phosphate • Insulin and Oral
Hypoglycemic Drugs • Chromium Piccolinate • Amino
Acid Supplements

*Chapter 6*   **GETTING PUMPED**   102
Cocaine • Amphetamine • Ephedrine (Ma Huang, "Herbal
Ecstasy") • Ritalin • Bronchodilators • Decongestants •
Caffeine • Blood Doping and EPO

*Chapter 7*   **CHILLING OUT: ALCOHOL AND MARIJUANA**   129

*Chapter 8*   **SMOKING AND CHEWING: TOBACCO**   150

*Chapter 9*   **COOLING DOWN**   160
Valium and Other Sedatives • Kava Kava • GHB and
GHL • Painkillers • Natural Opiates • Beta Blockers •
Prozac and Its Friends

*Bibliography*   171

*Index*   181

We acknowledge the enthusiastic help of Duke
students in our classes, and particularly George Spanos,
for help in collecting information for this book.

# PUMPED

# INTRODUCTION

Our culture is increasingly obsessed with physical appearance and performance. Athletes are among the wealthiest and most revered people in the public eye. The media teaches us that beauty and strength are our major playing cards in life, and everybody wants to be athletic and attractive. No wonder people would do anything, including risking their lives, to be among the strong and the beautiful. For professional athletes the rewards are enormous, and there are tremendous incentives to do anything to win. The average Olympic gold medal in a marquis sport is worth a fortune in endorsements, and the publicity leading to hero status is intoxicating. There are powerful motives for taking substances that might give you the extra punch needed to hit the big time. The combination of money in athletics and the desire of everyone to be beautiful has led to a huge market in drugs and supplements.

An impressive array of chemicals is sold to enhance performance, with the advertising splattered across magazines, radio, TV. Now, Internet Web sites advertise various performance-enhancing substances for sale, no questions asked. Some of these drugs are effective but dangerous. Some are simply not effective and therefore a waste of money. Still, there is a slow and steady spread of drug use from the professional athletes' world to the world of amateur sports, even to students in middle and high school. Some kids begin using anabolic steroids before they even hit puberty.

We wrote this book because information is power. Anyone involved in sports should understand what the body needs to perform at its best and how the available performance-enhancing drugs and supplements really affect health and physical accomplishment. We talk about what works and what doesn't, what's safe, what's risky, and how to know the difference.

We also talk about the ways that recreational drugs affect performance. Although no one seriously considers these to be performance enhancing, many athletes use them without realizing how much they can impair performance. We think that smart and mature athletes who read this book will choose not to use these drugs and that the kind of trustworthy information we provide here will help young people make the same decision.

The first four chapters provide basic information describing how the body works and how drugs affect it. This is basic information everyone needs to know. Next, we turn to the drugs and techniques commonly used in an effort to enhance performance and training. Finally, we discuss some recreational drugs.

Every statement in this book is backed by published fact. This is not a series of scare stories but rather the straight dope about how chemicals improve and impair performance and the price an athlete pays for using them, as far as the current research reveals.

Chapter 1

# OPTIMIZING

# PERFORMANCE

## CONTENTS

The Brain: Sensing, Organizing, and Initiating Movement

The Heart, Circulatory System, and Lungs: Delivering Oxygen and Glucose

Muscles: What Creates Strength?

Energy for Muscle Movement: Eat to Move

Energy from Food: Carbohydrates, Fats, and Proteins

*Sugars*

*Fats*

*Proteins*

Energy Stores in the Muscle

Fatigue

Training: What Changes?

The Bottom Line

Faster, stronger, harder: everybody who works out or competes, from the afternoon jogger to the elite athlete, wants to run faster, keep going longer, or lift more weight. Among elite athletes for whom success can mean wealth and fame, the stakes can be very high. Even the aging jogger trying to "keep up" with younger competition may be strongly motivated to seek an extra boost.

In a society that has accepted the use of chemicals to cure disease, modify mood, change personality, and create recreation, it seems natural to turn to chemicals to improve athletic performance. Yet most people can't judge whether a chemical will achieve the desired results, whether it will just cost money, or whether it will cause harm. This is an ideal environment for those who market such chemicals because uninformed people are gullible customers.

The purpose of this chapter is to provide a simple view of what the body needs to train and perform optimally, so we can weigh the effectiveness and safety of particular drugs in later chapters. More importantly, having a grip on this kind of information allows you to judge future claims made by ingenious salespeople. Our focus will be on the brain; the circulatory system; the lungs; the liver and fat, which provide energy; and the muscles, which produce the work of movement. These are the essential organs on which every athlete depends.

# The Brain: Sensing, Organizing, and Initiating Movement

For each of us, the brain directs all movement in a marvelous and coordinated symphony. Sensory information from the eyes, ears, and joints tells the brain where your body is in space, how fast it is moving, and what oxygen and energy it needs. Your brain makes the decision to move, then signals the muscles to contract in the appropriate pattern. This happens both for automatic processes (like breathing) and for intentional movements. The information is carried from the brain by nerve fibers to the spinal cord first, which then relays them to other nerve cells and finally to the muscles.

The autonomic nervous system is a part of the brain that athletes often ignore, but it is critical to performance. It's an organization of nerves that travel to the heart, the lungs, and internal organs to regulate and control the systems that move oxygen and blood. It's called *autonomic* because these actions all take place automatically, without conscious control. This is how your heart rate increases during exercise and slows during rest, how the breathing tubes in your lungs widen during exercise, and how your liver releases glucose for use as an energy source for the muscles. Drugs can affect all of these processes. For example, stimulants like cocaine and ephedrine arouse the autonomic nervous system, making the heart and lungs act as if one is exercising even at rest.

During exercise, the brain responds to the need for oxygen by signaling the diaphragm to contract more frequently. Thus you breathe faster. All of these actions happen without you even thinking about it. In contrast, voluntary movements begin with intention. Then both the automatic and conscious parts of the brain work together to send signals to the muscles to contract and relax in a smooth and precise way. As the muscles move, your brain also processes feedback about the results of its signals. Nerves connecting the muscles and joints to the brain provide information about the position of joints in space and about the extent to which muscles have been stretched. The brain uses this information reflexively to maintain the position of the body. For you to train or perform complex or strenuous activity, your brain must be working at its best, both in its automatic control of breathing and heartbeat, in its voluntary control of muscle, and in its awareness of how you are moving through space.

People often contrast *brain*, meaning intellect, and *brawn*, meaning physical strength and performance. In reality, brawn is useless without the brain. You may have heard the expression "The most important sex organ is the brain." Well, the same is true for physical performance. The brain is the most essential player. You can attain a reasonable level of performance with limited muscle strength, limited energy supplies, and even with some physical handicaps. But you can't perform at all unless the control systems in the brain are working well. Not only is the brain the most crucial and complex player, it is without doubt the most underappreciated component of athletic performance. Athletes who want to perform at their best need to care for their brains with the same rigor with which they care for their hearts and their muscles.

## The Heart, Circulatory System, and Lungs: Delivering Oxygen and Glucose

For muscles to work, they need oxygen and energy, in the form of glucose (sugar) or fat. The lungs deliver the oxygen to the bloodstream. Each person has a particular lung volume that is determined genetically and can't be changed. No matter how much you train, the amount of air your lungs are capable of holding remains the same. But the width of the tubes through which air moves from your mouth into your lungs is variable. Neural and hormonal messages stimulate the muscle to widen or narrow these passages, called *bronchioles*. If the restriction of air flow severely limits an athlete's ability to exercise (as in asthma), certain drugs like albuterol (Chapter 6) can be used to relax the muscle and widen the bronchioles. Some athletes need to use these to be able to exercise at all.

Once the blood is oxygenated, the heart pumps it to its final destination through the blood vessels. The basic size of the heart and its ability to pump effectively are determined genetically. However, the autonomic nervous system controls how fast the heart beats and where blood goes in the body. The amount of blood flowing to a particular part of your body is regulated in a matter of seconds by the ability of blood vessels to narrow or widen. For example, when you exercise, your body temperature rises due to your increased use of energy. Your autonomic nervous system widens the blood vessels in your skin to allow blood to pass near the surface of the skin where heat dissipates. It also causes the blood vessels in the muscles to widen to deliver more oxygen. After a meal, it directs blood to the intestines to allow rapid absorption of nutrients. As you can imagine, if you try to exercise immediately after eating, your body gets a set of conflicting directions because your autonomic nervous system is trying to send blood on two simultaneous missions: absorb nutrients and oxygenate the muscles.

## Muscles: What Creates Strength?

Muscle is composed of fibers attached to bone by tendons. Any muscle can only contract to shorten or relax to lengthen, thus moving the bones to which it is attached. Muscles have two kinds of strands within them that are different widths—thick and thin. At rest, thick and thin filaments in a muscle just barely overlap each other. Muscles shorten when these fibers slide to overlap each other in cycles of attaching and detaching. The movement is like a person climbing a rope. Larger muscles, containing more and bigger fibers, can move their attached bones against a greater resistance and/or faster. This is muscle strength.

Nerves cause movement by directing the shortening of muscle fibers. The nerves start in the spinal cord and travel out to the muscles, where they release a chemical called *acetylcholine*. This chemical triggers the release of calcium in the muscle cells, and the calcium then initiates a complex series of chemical events inside the muscle.

Muscles are not all the same; some are made for bursts of activity that are short-lived, while others are made for long-lasting activities. The fast-twitch fibers shorten quickly and are activated easily for brief activities like sprinting. These fibers can respond quickly but not for very long because they don't have the cellular machinery for prolonged energy production. They fatigue quickly. Slow-twitch fibers, on the other hand, respond slowly but can keep going for a long time, and they generate force for prolonged periods of exercise like cycling or long-distance running.

No doubt you've noticed that some people are naturally better at sprintlike activities whereas others are likely to succeed at more prolonged activities. One reason is that our genes determine the ratio of fast- to slow-twitch fibers in various muscles. Training can make your muscle fibers work more efficiently, but training does not substantially change the ratio of fast- to slow-twitch fibers. Training clearly increases the *size* of each muscle fiber. We are less certain about whether training increases the *number* of fibers. Some studies show that body builders with big legs have more muscle fibers in them than normal people, but we don't know if they just started out with more or if the specific kind of exercise triggered formation of new fibers. Other sorts of training like running or simple weight lifting mainly increase the size of individual fibers.

## Energy for Muscle Movement: Eat to Move

Moving muscle fibers requires lots of energy that is provided by a molecule called *adenosine triphosphate* (ATP). ATP is the basic "energy currency" of the body. It comes from the breakdown of sugar to carbon dioxide and water and is used for energy everywhere in the body, including muscles. However, it is heavy, and rather than store it, the body continuously makes it.

The breakdown of sugar to make ATP occurs in two phases. The first part of this process goes quickly and does not require oxygen. This is called *anaerobic* (without oxygen) *metabolism*. It does not produce much ATP (about 5 percent of the total use of a glucose molecule for energy), but it makes it fast. A sprinting athlete relies on anaerobic metabolism.

The second part of this process, the part that burns oxygen, is called *aerobic metabolism*. This produces energy during sustained exercise and for most cellular work in the body. Aerobic metabolism provides the energy for running a marathon, swimming a mile, or cycling in the Tour de France.

## Energy from Food: Carbohydrates, Fats, and Proteins

The chemical energy for making ATP comes from carbohydrates and fats that we get from our diets. When we eat, food is broken down into its component parts: carbohydrates into simple sugars like glucose, fats into simple molecules called *fatty acids*, and proteins into their building blocks called *amino acids*.


## SUGARS


Most of the sugars and carbohydrates we eat come as sugar molecules linked together in a form called *starch*. However, up to 25 percent of carbohydrate in the American diet comes from simple sugar (sucrose) itself: sodas, sugar on cereal, etc. When we eat, starch is broken down in the digestive system into simple sugars that are just single molecules or two sugar molecules linked together. These sugar molecules enter the bloodstream, then go directly to the liver. Although there are many kinds of sugar molecules (for example, table sugar is a molecule of glucose linked to a molecule of fructose), our body can use only glucose. Any other sugars that we eat are converted into glucose by the liver and stored in a long string of glucose molecules, called *glycogen*. About one-quarter of the body's glycogen is in the liver. The remainder is in muscles, where it is broken down, and the glucose is used for energy during exercise.

Glycogen is a rapidly used energy source, but there isn't all that much of it. A normal body contains about 2,000 calories as glycogen—enough for a single 20-mile run. In fact, all the glycogen in the liver can be used up in an intense two-hour workout. It provides the fuel at the beginning of exercise and during exercise at high intensity, but it is not the energy storehouse of the body (more about this below). It's good that we don't have a lot of glycogen because glycogen is relatively laden with the "empty" weight of water. For every 10 grams of glycogen, the body must store almost 30 grams of water.

"Carbohydrate loading" is the practice of eating a diet high in sugars some period of time (typically three days) before an athletic event. "Carbo-loading" does improve performance in sustained, aerobic events like marathons or cycling races, but it doesn't help for shorter, more intense events. Optimal carbohydrate loading occurs when an athlete does a long, sustained exercise bout to deplete glycogen (for example, a 20-mile training run), and then spends the next three days replacing it by eating a diet high in carbohydrates (70 percent). A single high-carbohydrate meal the night before a competition provides some glycogen storage but less than the several day strategy described above. Any form of carbohydrate is effective, although complex carbohydrates work best. During an event, simple sugars (as in sugar-containing drinks) are much more useful because there isn't time to break down complex carbohydrates into glucose. The muscle uses these sugars directly and spares the remaining glycogen.

## FATS

The title of "energy storehouse" belongs to fat. In contrast to the one pound of glycogen in our bodies, about 12 percent of a normal man's body weight is fat (that's about 18 pounds of fat for a 150 pound man). A normal woman's body is about 25 percent fat (that's 30 pounds of fat for a 120 pound woman).

Despite our cultural obsession to avoid fat, it provides most of the fuel for low-intensity and prolonged exercise. Fat is broken down into its constituent molecules, called *fatty acids*, which go to the muscles and the liver. Fat is an incredibly efficient way to store energy. It's light, it doesn't store much water (unlike glycogen), and its every molecule has a high energy capacity. Many neural and hormonal signals regulate the breakdown of fat to convert it to energy. Of course many people would like to take a "fat-burning" drug that would simply dissolve fat. However, fat burning is a complex biochemical process, and there is no such drug—no matter what people claim (see Chapter 4).

## PROTEINS

Protein is broken down into its constituent parts, called *amino acids*, during the process of digestion. Amino acids are taken up and sent to all cells in the body, where they serve as the building blocks for synthesis of the proteins in our own cells. A small amount of these amino acids in the body can be converted into glucose, but usually amino acids are not a major energy source. The amino acids that protein provides are much more important for building proteins than as an energy source. Does this mean that taking *amino acid supplements* will help you build muscle? Read on in Chapter 5. The answer may surprise you.

## Energy Stores in the Muscle

Just a few seconds of intense exercise can use up all the ATP present in a muscle. *Creatine phosphate* is the next energy source to be tapped (see Chapter 5). There is not a tremendous amount of creatine phosphate stored in muscle, but there is more than ATP. Because creatine is an energy source, it is becoming increasingly popular as a nutritional supplement to prolong exercise tolerance. The problem is that it lasts just slightly longer than the stored ATP: about ten seconds. Therefore, creatine can help you only for a very short while.

Once creatine phosphate is used up, the muscle needs to burn fuel to create more ATP for energy. *Anaerobic metabolism* (without oxygen) gets you from about ten seconds to about two minutes (a 200-yard sprint or a 100-meter swim). It is fast but short-lived, and at a very high intensity of work anaerobic metabolism can't keep up with the energy demands made by the muscle. The muscle fatigues, and movement slows down. Marathons, cycling, and other distance events—or any form of exercise that lasts longer than a couple of minutes—requires the richer but slower process of *aerobic metabolism*. The source of energy for aerobic metabolism depends on how long you are exercising, and how hard you are exercising. During a 3 to 4-mile jog, or any sustained aerobic task that lasts less than an hour, about one-third of the energy used comes from fat, about one-third from glucose, and about one-third from energy sources in the muscle. The longer you extend this activity, the more you burn fat. For example, after four hours of sustained aerobic exercise, fat provides at least 70 percent of your energy requirements. Imagine how much fat is being burned during an Iron Man triathlon, which can last up to twelve hours.

## Fatigue

The simplest reason for fatigue is that muscles run out of ATP and don't have the energy supply to keep contracting. To keep exercising, muscles must have a supply of glucose and oxygen, plus time to remake ATP. This is the premise of interval training, in which you do a burst of activity, then allow some time for recovery. Also, as you exercise, lactic acid builds up and contributes to fatigue. The increase in lactic acid affects many processes in muscle, including key energy-producing enzymes and the ability of muscle to contract.

Something many people don't know is that lactic acid can have significant effects on the brain. It can cause feelings of anxiety, even panic. In fact, physicians use injections of lactic acid to test people for panic disorder. At a high enough level of effort, the combination of high oxygen demand and lactic-acid increase may make some people feel really bad. Yet it is part of fatigue and its chemical consequences in your brain. This can be minimized by gradually increasing the intensity of training over many days—as we discuss in the next section.

## Training: What Changes?

The purpose of training is to make specific actions more coordinated, faster, and easier. What changes with training? Everything! Regular training causes adaptations in every bodily function involved in exercise. It improves the delivery of oxygen to the exercising muscle, the efficiency with which the muscle generates and uses energy, the ability of the cardiovascular system to deliver energy and oxygen, and, finally, the ability of the brain to direct efficient movements. The principle of training is simple: Repeating an exercise over and over again triggers adaptive changes in each part of the body put under stress by the exercise. Those adaptive changes lead to better performance.

Even the brain and central nervous system change with training, although we don't know how. The nerves that direct specific muscles actually do so faster. Breathing is more efficient and deeper. Motion is initiated more quickly. Most important, learning is a big part of the training for complex sports. Given the complicated motions involved in a pole vault, or a racing start off the blocks into the swimming pool, the most important changes that occur with training for these activities don't happen in the muscles but in the brain. Anything that impairs learning will impair training.

Everybody knows that muscles get bigger when they are exercised. The muscle makes more fibers, individual muscle fibers get bigger, and then the muscle can generate more force, or *tension*. Generally, only the muscles that are exercised get bigger. This is one limitation to the idea of "cross-training"—engaging in several different forms of exercise to promote general fitness. It might help with the heart and lungs, but it won't help with the muscles unless you use the same ones every time. Generally, sprinting stresses fast-twitch muscle, so fast-twitch muscles undergo the greatest changes. Similarly, long-term aerobic exercise, like cycling or running, puts the most stress on slow-twitch fibers, so they change the most.

Does training actually change the ratio of fast-twitch to slow-twitch muscle? Can a distance runner become a sprinter? Not very successfully. Some changes do occur, but generally you are stuck with the ratio encoded in your genes. However, even a slow jogger can improve her sprinting by practicing sprinting, putting stress on her fast-twitch fibers to improve her performance.

Training causes other changes in muscles that are just as important as creating more muscle fibers. Muscles actually make more mitochondria (the place inside the cell that aerobic metabolism takes place) and even grow new capillaries to deliver blood and oxygen more efficiently. These changes help the muscles generate more energy. Other, more specific changes depend upon the particular training that you choose. When you train for sprinting, the biggest changes occur in the processes that are required for short-term energy bursts (anaerobic metabolism). During long-lasting aerobic training, like a daily jog or bike ride, the enzymes required for sustained production of energy in the presence of oxygen (aerobic metabolism) increase. These changes are far more productive over the long run than the ingestion of specific nutrients like creatine that are designed to improve energy production. One big unknown about the use of supplements like creatine during training is whether they will slow or prevent the normal adaptive changes that muscles make. Your exercising body needs to notice its natural energy shortages as they occur in order to adapt in a way that improves performance. Providing these energy "fillers" artificially will deprive the body of this information and reduce the benefits of training.

The cardiovascular system also changes during training. Here is where cross-training really can help because anything that puts a demand on the heart to pump faster to deliver more oxygen will bring about these adaptations. Cross-training accomplishes several things. First, the heart gets a little bigger, and each beat of the heart pumps more blood into the circulation. Second, the actual blood volume as well as the number of oxygen-carrying red blood cells increases. Third, blood flow gets diverted to the exercising muscles more efficiently with training. And although the size of your lungs doesn't change, you breathe more efficiently, so after training, the amount of air you breathe in and out in a given period of time is actually larger.

## The Bottom Line

1. The brain is the most important organ in the body for exercise. It directs movement, sends blood to the muscle, and speeds up breathing.

2. Different kinds of exercise use different energy stores. Stored ATP and creatine last about five to ten seconds; anaerobic metabolism lasts up to several minutes. Aerobic metabolism is the workhorse that provides energy for sustained, submaximal exercise for hours.
3. Glucose from glycogen breakdown in muscles and the liver provides energy for anaerobic metabolism and for aerobic metabolism. This store runs out in a couple of hours.
4. The longer exercise continues, the more fat contributes to the energy supply.
5. Fatigue develops when lactic acid builds up in the muscle and energy supplies are exhausted. This happens in a couple of minutes at high intensity, but not for hours with low-intensity effort.
6. Training improves each of these functions: the brain, the cardiovascular and pulmonary systems that deliver oxygen, production of energy for exercise, as well as muscle size and strength.

The important judgment that every athlete needs to make about *any* drug or supplement is whether it provides any significant benefit compared to the benefit of serious training—and whether it might even *prevent* normal training effects.

Chapter 2

# HOW TO READ
# THE ADS

## CONTENTS

What Is Improvement?

How to Evaluate Claims for Improvement

*Go Buy Those Amino Acid Supplements Now?*

*The Trouble with Tribulus*

Is It Worth It?

The Bottom Line

It should be easy to show that an athlete swims or runs faster, lifts more weight, or exercises longer in response to a particular substance. Proving that drugs and supplements improve performance is not as easy as it sounds. Advertising, books, even talks and reports by experts, are full of stories about how performance is improved by this or that strategy. Many drugs are touted because they seem to change body composition (to decrease fat, increase muscle bulk, etc.). However, such changes don't necessarily translate into improved performance. A drug that increases water content in the muscles will seem to "pump up" lean body mass. If you are a body builder and your goal is improved appearance, that might be fine with you. But if the goal is improved strength or endurance, such a change doesn't mean anything.

## What Is Improvement?

First you must choose your goals. Are you aiming to improve appearance, size, or performance? Then you must decide how much improvement is acceptable. Do you want to lift twice as much weight as before or to cycle for 40 percent longer? It is highly unlikely that you would get that kind of improvement from any drug now on the market. When a drug or supplement is reported to "work" in the scientific literature, the effect may be as small as a 5 percent improvement because scientific studies measure change in statistical terms. While 5 percent may not mean much for the week-end warrior, it could be career making for the elite runner or swim-mer. So when you hear that a drug improves performance, remember that the size of the effect may or may not count for you.

Athletes use performance-enhancing drugs for two different reasons. First, they enhance the body's response to training. Ana-bolic agents like testosterone are supposed to work with rather than replace the effects of training. One concern about creatine, on the other hand, is that it may load the muscle with creatine but prevent the normal adaptations by which the trained muscle produces more on its own. Unfortunately, this has not been tested.

Second, some athletes use drugs (illegally) to improve perfor-mance during competition. Such drugs include stimulants to improve endurance in aerobic events. In addition to raising a legal/moral issue of unfair advantage, this kind of drug use can cause injury or death by placing extra burden on a maximally stressed body.

Here are the sorts of changes that most athletes want to gain from training and any other aid to training or performance, from sleep practices to foods to drugs.

*Improvements to Fitness/Performance*
- Altered body composition: increased lean body mass, decreased body fat
- Increased strength in particular muscles
- Increase in measures of aerobic capacity: maximal oxygen uptake
- Faster time to complete events (swimming, running)
- Increased weight lifted
- Longer time to exhaustion

## How to Evaluate Claims for Improvement

How does a nonscientist judge claims of improved performance? There are some easy guidelines. Don't believe "satisfied consumer" testimonials, and be skeptical of advertising claims on bottles. "Scientific studies" should be mentioned in a way that you can find them at a library: the author and/or journal should be mentioned. You don't need to look them up necessarily, but if someone is not afraid for you to look at the results, they are probably legitimate.

Studies conducted in animals are a start, but it's very difficult to extrapolate from these studies to human experience. Human studies should involve more than just a few subjects, and they should show "statistically significant" improvements in some performance measure that makes sense. Reading the titles of articles published about performance-enhancing practices can be very encouraging until you look at the number of people included in the study, often as few as four to eight. Such articles should also mention the size of the change they claim to have observed, so you can judge whether such an "enhancement" or "benefit" is worth your while.

Many nutritional supplements now contain combinations of ephedrine and/or caffeine and aspirin, and they cite research showing weight loss from this treatment in obese patients. What the blurbs don't tell you is the amount of weight loss—usually only about 10 pounds over several months. Still, these were studies in humans, with reasonable numbers of people under study, and the research findings were published in the scientific literature; so far so good in terms of reliability. So if your goal is to

## Go Buy Those Amino Acid Supplements Now?

A study was just published in a high-quality scientific journal, showing that consumption of a particular amino acid after exercise improved muscle protein synthesis. The author concluded that an athlete in training should eat 111 to 159 grams of protein daily, well above even the high estimates given by most nutritionists. Where did the scientists come up with this number? Frankly, we aren't sure. It involves some very big assumptions. First of all, the study used rats, and the rats were starved going into the exercise regimen—a good way to observe the most dramatic changes but not a good way to replicate the environment of a well-fed athlete. Second, the subjects were given just the one amino acid. There was no comparison involving a normal mixture of amino acids, comparable to a high-protein diet. Finally, the experimental subjects were sedentary animals. Would you run out and take a supplement of amino acid on the basis of this claim? We hope not—unless you are a starved and inactive rodent.

shed that last 10 pounds before summer or the last few pounds before a competition, and you have the time to do it, then this might be a sensible enough treatment to try. But these supplements are not going to melt 50 pounds from an obese frame overnight, nor are they likely to make much of a difference to anyone in a demanding exercise program, which is a much more efficient way to lose weight.

Before you take any scientific study to heart, you should check to see if the study involved subjects like you. If you are middle-aged, out of shape, and starting an aerobic exercise regimen, then results from studies of people who are unfit are the results that matter. If you are an elite athlete, then these studies might not have any meaning for you. Instead, you should look for studies of trained athletes on maximal exercise regimens.

## Kinds of Evidence Used to Support Manufacturer's Claims

### Poor
- Consumer testimonials
- Advertising brochures
- Manufacturer's information

### Potentially Flawed
- Individual case reports
- Studies involving small numbers of experimental subjects
- Studies using people who never exercise or are just starting an exercise program
- Studies providing no specifics about the experimental details

### Credible Studies
- Use appropriately selected subjects (trained athletes or suitable target population)
- Involve adequate numbers of subjects (typically fifteen to twenty, not four or five)
- Provide exact details of treatment
- Use doses that seem reasonable
- Provide comparison subjects who do not receive the drug or supplement
- Conduct statistical analysis of the data

## The Trouble with Tribulus

Tribulus Terrestris is an ancient Chinese and Indian herbal medicine that has been used for diseases ranging from heart troubles to impotence. Ads tout "scientific research" showing that it increases testosterone levels 30 to 50 percent. The ads have the mechanisms right—Tribulus is supposed to increase production of luteinizing hormone from the pituitary gland, stimulating the body's own mechanisms for producing testosterone. Yet, credible medical research literature about this herb reports only that grazing animals that eat too much Tribulus become hypersensitive to light and prone to movement disorders. Certain molecules in the plant can help some forms of heart disease, but unfortunately other molecules can damage the nervous systems of experimental animals.

The "scientific research" cited by advertisers consists of a single report in a supplement guide, and the Web-published research of a Bulgarian pharmaceutical company that markets it (under the name Tribestan) for impotence and infertility. According to that story, Tribulus did "increase testosterone 30 percent." However, this research did not indicate the variability from person to person in the testosterone measures. Even if the individual responses were consistent, a 30 percent rise is probably not significant for a normal man. A man's testosterone receptors are completely full at normal levels, so even a 30 percent increase accomplishes little. Testosterone levels of people who took Tribulus in the trials were still more or less normal even after the drug. Only levels vastly in excess of normal (a 1,000–10,000 percent increase) can stimulate greater muscle deposition in a normal man. That doesn't mean taking vast quantities of Tribulus will achieve this, and ingesting large amounts could have all kinds of negative effects we don't know about yet.

Can Tribulus jump-start testes that are atrophied from steroid use? Maybe, but there is no evidence of significant effects over the long run. So far we don't know what Tribulus does in women. In large amounts, it could potentially disrupt a woman's menstrual cycle. This is an untested plant product with many chemicals in it, and there are no long-term safety studies or any governmental quality control on Tribulus preparations.

## Is It Worth It?

Finally, the athlete must consider whether the benefit is worth any long-term risks from the drug or supplement. This information often is not available. Many studies use doses in an appropriate range for a medical treatment rather than the larger doses that athletes are likely to use. For example, doses of anabolic steroids that increase testosterone levels within the normal range may have no long-term hazards. However, athletes who use vastly larger doses may be in danger. Remember that many scientific studies are conducted as a single trial, under ideal conditions, or for a brief period of time.

### Considerations for Long-Term Safety
- Are the doses used the same as those used by athletes?
- Does use of the supplement during training prevent natural adaptations to training?

- Does use of the supplement in a competitive setting offer particular hazards?
- Are there effects on other bodily functions—reproduction, for example? How readily are these changes reversed?
- How long must treatments be considered: have treatments this long been tested?

What would we consider an acceptable performance-enhancing substance? A *legal* substance that (1) improves performance without preventing normal training-related adaptations, (2) is backed by multiple, high-quality scientific studies in an appropriate population, and (3) poses no long-term health risks to the athlete at the customary doses.

Most drugs don't meet these criteria. Some are simply ineffective. Virtually all the effective drugs have some risks, ranging from slight and temporary (muscle cramping from taking creatine) to major and lifelong (voice changes and/or permanent changes in genitalia in women taking anabolic steroids). For most drugs, the long-term consequences are unknown. Many athletes play this dangerous game without knowing the rules.

## The Bottom Line

1. Athletes know what they want: more strength, more aerobic capacity, less fat.
2. You need to judge claims carefully, whether they're in an ad or a scientific study.
3. Weigh the risks! Supplements that seem too good to be true probably are.

Chapter 3

# WARMING UP

## Drug Basics

### CONTENTS

What Is a Drug?
How Do Drugs Work?
*Premature Puberty Due to a Skin Cream*
The Effects of Drugs Change over Time
*Why Athletes Get Caught for Using Nandrolone*
Drugs and the Brain: A Special Case
   *Addiction*
The Bottom Line

# What Is a Drug?

A drug is any substance taken to change mental state or bodily function. Vitamins, herbal preparations, pills prescribed by a physician, over-the-counter cold remedies, veterinary drugs for horses, coffee, and beer are all drugs. A drug can be a natural part of the body like an element, a plant product, or a synthetic chemical. Products marketed as "natural" still change how your body works, so they are still drugs. Ephedrine, a drug used by some athletes to lose weight, provides a great example. The molecule ephedrine exists in plants and can be ingested as an herbal tea, as a pill used to treat asthma, or as a single component of a combination preparation marketed for "fat burning." It is still the same drug, and it affects the body in the same way.

Drugs don't necessarily improve how the body works. Sometimes they're used to cure disease, sometimes they're used to make a normal body abnormal, and sometimes they're used to improve a normal body. Here are three examples. Penicillin is an antibiotic that kills bacteria and cures infection. It clearly belongs in the first category. Birth control pills fit the second category, making a normal woman temporarily infertile. This achieves a desired clinical effect, but it does not cure disease or improve how the body works. The third category includes supplements and drugs used by athletes to enhance performance or appearance.

Most of the drugs to be discussed in this book fit the third and most controversial category: drugs intended to make a normal body better.

Can this really be done? If you take a vitamin supplement, are you improving your body's natural makeup—improving its resistance to colds or the effects of aging, for example? Most physiologists would question this. If you are vitamin or mineral deficient, there is no question that you can improve your health by taking vitamins. Many adolescent girls don't get enough calcium from dietary sources alone, especially if they don't drink milk at every meal, so taking calcium supplements makes a lot of sense. Furthermore, if you are a heavily training athlete, it is possible that you lose more specific nutrients than the average person and so need to take more. However, taking more than you need doesn't help. If you're lucky, the body just gets rid of the excess, and you've wasted your money but not damaged your health. Sometimes this approach can backfire more seriously by leading to toxic levels of drugs. Selenium is a good example. Selenium is an element that your body needs in tiny amounts to work correctly, and enterprising marketers have used this information to market selenium supplements aggressively. But selenium is toxic in excessive amounts. So taking supplements can actually make your health worse, not better.

## How Do Drugs Work?

Generally, the more of a drug someone takes, the bigger the effect. However, all bodily systems reach a maximum. Drugs act by attaching to specific places on cells called *receptors*, but there are always a finite number of receptors for each drug. Therefore, taking more drug than there are receptors is pointless. The excess drug circulates in the body until it is eliminated without having beneficial effects. Or the excess drug produces unwanted side effects.

Drugs must get to their receptors in order to act. In most cases this means getting into the blood. Injecting a drug intravenously is the quickest, most efficient, and most dangerous way of getting it into the bloodstream. Drug levels in the circulation reach their peak in a minute or two, and most drugs easily enter any tissue from the bloodstream. Drugs can also be injected directly into the muscle or just under the skin. This is a little slower because the drug must leave the site of injection and enter a blood vessel to be distributed throughout the body. Injecting a drug is unpleasant, requires special sterile equipment, and involves considerable danger of infection. It also greatly increases the risk of overdose, associated with high levels of the drug in the body. Athletes who inject insulin face the danger of lowering their blood sugar too far or too quickly.

Inhaling drugs into the lungs can deliver a drug almost as quickly to the circulation as intravenous injection. Many drugs used to treat asthma, like albuterol, are delivered this way. In this case, inhaling the drug is ideal because it is delivered directly to the place that needs it. Smokers also use this route to deliver nicotine to the brain. The surface area of the lungs is very large, and the blood supply of the lungs goes directly to the heart and then out to the other tissues. Therefore, smoking some drugs delivers them to the tissues almost as quickly as intravenous injection.

Some drugs can enter the body through the mucous membranes in the nose, mouth, vagina, or rectum. The mucous membranes are thinner than skin, and drugs enter more easily. Drugs that can cross cell membranes and enter the brain generally can pass through mucous membranes. Athletes who chew tobacco or do snuff use this route to get nicotine into the body.

The most common way that people get drugs into their system is to swallow them. Drugs that are swallowed pass through the walls of the stomach or intestine, then enter the capillaries, which drain through the liver before going to the heart. This process takes time, so swallowing a drug is the easiest but slowest way to

## Premature Puberty Due to a Skin Cream

A few drugs, those that move easily through fat, can be absorbed through the skin. A recent study reported an amazing example of this. A toddler entered puberty because of his father's anabolic steroid cream. It seems that dad was an avid weight lifter and also a fond parent. Because of the skin-to-skin contact between father and son, plus the son's contact with dad's mats and other equipment, the son absorbed enough testosterone through his skin to start going through puberty while still a toddler! His penis started growing, and he developed facial hair.

get a drug into the body. If you're trying to stop an asthma attack, then this matters. However, if you're trying to deliver a drug to aid protein synthesis, split-second timing isn't really necessary.

Many ads in body-building magazines tout effervescent preparations that get drugs into the body faster. But when trying to load the muscle with creatine over days, what does it matter if a single dose gets into the muscle in fifteen minutes or thirty minutes? Even if you want to promote protein synthesis after a workout, a difference in timing doesn't mean much because the process takes hours. Effervescent preparations (in which the active ingredients dissolve quickly in water) can be easily absorbed, but they usually cost more, and the increased cost likely outweighs the enhanced absorption.

Most drugs are effective in pill form. Some, like growth hormone, are proteins and are digested in the stomach and thus inactivated. These drugs must be injected. There are many supplements of growth hormone, luteinizing hormone, thyroid-stimulating hormone, and the like in pill form that will not work. These drugs are all proteins that the stomach will destroy.

The liver and the kidneys cooperate to remove drugs from the body. The liver converts many drugs to forms that the kidneys can then excrete. Drugs don't "hide" in certain places in the body, although this is a common myth. But some drugs like steroids are easily stored in fat and may be slowly released into the circulation long after they were first absorbed.

## The Effects of Drugs Change over Time

Drugs don't work forever. Many drugs cause much smaller reactions in the body after they have been taken for a while. At first

### Why Athletes Get Caught for Using Nandrolone

One of the most common drugs detected by drug testing at athletic events is the steroid nandrolone. This steroid, injected into a muscle in an oily solution that traps the drug, is gradually leaked into the circulation. Once there, the liver destroys it fairly rapidly. However, some of it is taken up into fat and stored. Then it takes the body weeks to get rid of it. Athletes who use this drug for illegal performance enhancement are often quite careful to stop using it weeks before competitions to compensate for its slow removal from the body. They often switch to a form of testosterone that is immediately available to the circulation, more easily destroyed by the liver, and eliminated faster.

many weight lifters experience big improvements from taking steroids, but then the rate of improvement slows down. The body builders often compensate by taking more, but eventually the improvements plateau, and even taking very high doses no longer helps. This change is called *tolerance.*

There are lots of reasons for tolerance. For one thing, there is an upper limit to what any body can achieve, despite maximally stimulating a receptor system. There are genetic limits to muscle growth in many people. So taking more and more steroids won't make everybody look like a body builder. In addition, all bodies tend to adapt to the presence of drugs, so bodily functions return to normal despite the presence of a drug. If a particular receptor system is stimulated over and over, eventually it starts to turn the signal off. If you take caffeine every day to increase alertness and break down fat, then eventually the body stops reacting to the caffeine.

Almost every system in the body can make this sort of adaptation. This is what limits the effectiveness of diet drugs. Some diet drugs decrease appetite by stimulating centers in the brain that make you think you are full. However, there are other centers in the brain that stimulate appetite when certain nutrients are not present. So when you take a diet drug every day, the drug keeps working on its receptor, continually making you think you are full when you aren't. In the meantime, the level of nutrients in your body decreases because you are eating less and less, which signals your brain to stimulate appetite more and more. You have created a war between two opposing centers in your brain. Eventually the hunger center will win out, and you'll start eating again, even though you're still taking a drug. For such vital functions as eating and breathing the body has many redundant safety systems to make sure that they keep working. When you upset the balance with a drug, the body tries to restore it.

# Drugs and the Brain: A Special Case

Only drugs that move easily through cell layers (like steroids) can enter the brain. Surprisingly, some other drugs that have become quite popular as stimulants really don't cross the barrier well. Athletes once used the stimulant amphetamine for performance enhancement. Amphetamine enters the brain very well, and it proved to be highly addictive. Now athletes use the asthma medicine ephedrine and the decongestant pseudoephedrine. Neither drug gets into the brain very well, and both lack many of the addicting effects of amphetamine.

Once drugs get into the brain, they act on receptors just like they do elsewhere in the body. The same receptors are used throughout the brain for many different purposes, from breathing to thinking, so it is very difficult to create a drug that affects just one kind of behavior. The most successful drugs are those that act on very specific receptors that have very few jobs. The ones that cause the most trouble, including alcohol and anesthetics, affect receptors that control everything the brain does.

## ADDICTION

Can you be addicted to steroids? To caffeine? To nutritional supplements in general? In order to answer these questions, we need to understand what addiction is. *Addiction is the process of compulsive, uncontrollable use of a drug, despite negative consequences.* This sounds pretty generic, and many people who actively seek any performance advantage, whether it be from chromium or anabolic steroids, may worry that they will get "addicted" to these drugs. Yet addiction is not as common a process as many people think. Everybody knows the major addictive drugs: nicotine; stimulants like cocaine and amphetamine, heroin, and other opiate drugs; and alcohol. We don't know yet whether marijuana and steroids really belong on this list.

These different drugs don't seem to have much in common. Cocaine makes you feel alert and euphoric, heroin makes you feel dreamy and relaxed, alcohol makes you relaxed and eventually sleepy. Nicotine seems to makes people a little more alert and perhaps calmer. They all stimulate the part of the brain that normally exists to help us enjoy life-sustaining activities, the reward system.

The reward system is the reason that sex feels good, that sweet and fatty foods taste good, and that so many people actively seek out new and unusual experiences. This is a very important part of what the brain does: it encourages us to engage in activities that are life or species sustaining. Research has shown that the drugs that are addictive directly activate this system—each one in a slightly different way. So taking cocaine stimulates some of the same systems in the brain that having sex stimulates. No wonder people develop a compulsive need for cocaine!

This view of addiction is pretty simplistic, and we need to add another wrinkle. The brain, like every other organ in the body, can develop tolerance. The reward system also adapts when it is over-stimulated, and research has shown many changes happen in the reward system when addictive drugs are present for long periods of time. In particular, it becomes less sensitive. Therefore, the drug user needs to take more and more drug to feel good, eventually only feeling good when the drug is present. If the drug is stopped, then even natural rewards like sex fail to satisfy the user. This lack of pleasure can also keep a drug user coming back for more. If you know that cocaine will make you feel great and that you'll feel terrible if you stop, then you have two reasons to keep using it.

Does this two-pronged process of reward and withdrawal apply to drugs that many body builders and other athletes use? This is a controversial question. There is no doubt that many anabolic steroid users notice that the minute they stop using steroids, their muscles start to shrink. Some athletes continue to use steroids to prevent this loss, even though they know that they are hurting their bodies. So they are continuing use in the presence of negative consequences— and some people would call that addiction. Furthermore, they do derive some indirect pleasure in terms of appearance. But we really don't have any evidence that taking anabolic steroids stimulates the reward system, so in that way it doesn't seem comparable to addictive "recreational" drugs. Yet anabolic steroids do get into the brain, and what they do there isn't well understood. The jury is still out.

Is a habit like compulsive vitamin taking an addiction? There is no evidence that your daily vitamin and mineral supplement directly affects brain activity, and certainly no evidence that vitamins or minerals stimulate the reward system. A superstitious ritual is not an addiction, though it can become a demanding habit. Many athletes have superstitious beliefs about training, nutrition, and substances. Some are based on a sound understanding of how the body works, while others are bunk. Nevertheless, the conviction that a particular practice helps is often all it takes. In pharmacology, we call this the "placebo effect," and it explains why even taking an inactive sugar pill can improve some symptoms of diseases. This is a real phenomenon, so if you think that a supplement helps, it might. The brain is that powerful.

## The Bottom Line

1. Drugs come in many forms: foods, pills, beverages, and herbs.
2. Drugs work on receptors. Drug effects are determined by what bodily functions are controlled by the receptors upon which they act. They rarely affect just one thing.
3. Only certain drugs can get into the brain. Once there, they act like other drugs and rarely affect just one behavior.

Chapter 4

# BULKING UP/
# SLIMMING DOWN

## CONTENTS

Basics about Food and Exercise

Losing Body Weight with Drugs

*Diuretics*

*Appetite Suppressants*

Purging and Vomiting

"Fat-Burning" Drugs

*Thyroid Hormone, or Triiodothyronine*

*DNP (Dinitrophenol)*

*Ephedrine and Other Stimulants*

*Caffeine and Theophylline*

"Fat-Blocking" Drugs

Special Issues for Women

*Putting It All Together: Burn Fat with Ephedrine and Caffeine?*

The Bottom Line

Every athlete seems to worry about body weight, one way or another—about being too slight, too heavy, not having enough muscle, having too much fat. Some athletes—dancers, gymnasts, and distance runners—are obsessed with maintaining low body weight because performance is optimized by leanness. In other sports like wrestling, athletes repeatedly lose weight in order to compete at a body weight below their natural weight. Other athletes like football players would do anything to add lean body mass that provides strength.

Many people have resorted to drugs or supplements to help them deal with their weight. Do any of these drugs work? Do nutritional supplements deliver what they promise—or just empty your wallet? A little common sense and a little knowledge about food and exercise is all you need to make these decisions for yourself.

## Basics about Food and Exercise

A simple magic formula explains body weight: body weight equals what goes in (food energy) minus what goes out (basal metabolism and exercise). It's like an hourglass, filling with sand (energy) at the top, emptying at the bottom with energy output. If you pour sand in faster than it goes out the other end by eating more food than you need, then the hourglass fills up, and you get fatter. If you balance input and output, then body weight doesn't change. If you increase output by increasing energy expenditure, then body weight falls. Given their high levels of exercise, many athletes in high intensity training have to struggle to keep their weight up.

Somewhere around 60 percent of the energy an average person burns in a day comes from basal metabolism and about 30 percent from exercise. The small remainder (about 10 percent) is the energy necessary to digest food. Body weight determines the amount of energy burned by basal metabolism. In all animals, from insects to elephants, the heavier an animal is, the more energy it expends—and the more it must eat!

Body composition and genetics also matter. The fitter a person is, the higher his metabolic rate. Some people are born with higher rates of metabolism than others, and gender also makes a difference. The basal metabolic rate of women is about 10 percent lower than that of men, partly due to differences in the percentages of body fat and muscle mass.

Dieting is a double-edged sword. As you reduce the intake of calories, the body becomes more efficient at using energy. It decreases energy consumption in order to survive. But if you're just trying to lose a few pounds, and not in danger of starving to death, it can be frustrating. As your body weight falls, you also expend less energy because your mass is smaller and your body is more efficient.

Exercise is the solution. Dieters who exercise do better because exercise burns calories and burns off fat. Exercise also builds muscles that use more energy than the same weight of fat. A recent (but controversial) scientific study proposed that people who tend to be thin simply burn more calories because they fidget! It's difficult to say how much energy use is attributable to fidgeting, but it is certainly true that the amount of energy you burn depends on what you do and how much effort you exert.

Anyone can increase his or her daily energy use by exercise. Light activities (activities during sitting, standing, or slowly moving around) burn about 120 to 150 calories per hour. Light to moderate activities (light gardening, washing a car, walking 1 to 3 miles per hour) use about 150 to 300 calories per hour. Walking faster (3½ to 4 miles per hour), heavier yard work, or dancing uses 300 to 400 calories per hour, while walking very fast (5 miles per hour), swimming, climbing, or shoveling snow use 400 to 600 calories per hour.

So even though basal metabolic rate contributes so much to energy use, lifestyle can have a tremendous impact. A person who lives a sedentary lifestyle spending most of the working day sitting or engaging in the activities described as "light" above uses only 20 percent more energy than her basal metabolic rate. A person who does heavy work for a living uses up to 50 percent more energy than her basal metabolic rate, or an additional 500 calories a day for a 130 pound woman.

*Energy consumption is determined by:*
   Body mass (bigger uses more)
   Percent lean body mass (muscle uses more than fat)
   Genetics
   Training (training makes your body more energy efficient)
   Dieting (dieting makes your body more energy efficient)

## Losing Body Weight with Drugs

### DIURETICS

Many athletes take diuretics to experience a quick loss of "water weight." Diuretics are drugs that decrease body weight by increasing urine output. Since the body loses only water, these drugs do *not* decrease body fat, and the weight loss is temporary. Use of diuretics is common in sports like wrestling, in which athletes compete in specific weight classes and often try to decrease their body weight before competition by any means possible. Jockeys who must also meet a target body weight before a horse race use the same strategy.

Diuretics interfere with the work of the kidneys, which filter the blood, removing waste and recapturing what is needed. Kidneys don't just remove waste, they also regulate the amount of fluid and salt in the body by controlling precisely how much salt and water are retained as they filter the blood. In the kidneys, as elsewhere in the body, water follows sodium (salt) through membranes due to a process called *osmosis*. So by controlling sodium, the kidneys control water movement, as well. If the body detects dehydration (like that occurring in a heavily exercising athlete who is sweating), the kidneys compensate by recapturing more sodium and retaining more water. This concentrates the urine. On the other hand, if the amount of water in the body is too high, the kidneys allow sodium to escape, water follows, and the urine becomes more dilute.

Diuretics are used in medical treatment to lower blood pressure by decreasing the amount of fluid in the circulation. When athletes take diuretics to lose weight, they lose water throughout the body, risking low blood pressure. In fact, horse trainers will give diuretics to a horse before a race specifically to lower the animal's blood pressure so as to prevent small hemorrhages in the lungs when the horse is giving its all. Fortunately, the effects of diuretics are temporary; as soon as the drug has left the bloodstream, the kidneys start to work normally again, and the body—animal or human—regains its lost fluid.

The use of diuretics to lose a few pounds before an event is not necessarily dangerous. On the other hand, if you take excessive doses or use the drug continuously, you'll find yourself dehydrated and low in potassium, which can make you dizzy, weak, lethargic, and nauseous. You could also find yourself experiencing potentially fatal disturbances of heart rhythm. Diuretics containing the drug furosemide can even make you deaf if you use them for a long time.

Recently, athletes have started using diuretics to dilute the urine before drug testing to prevent detection of performance-enhancing drugs. This is why most sports federations, including the United States Olympic Committee, have banned use of diuretics by athletes.

*Common diuretics banned by the United States Olympic Committee:*
   Amiloride (Midamor)
   Bendroflumethiazide (Naturetin)
   Benzthiazide (Aquatag, Exna, Hyrex, Marazide, Proaqua)
   Bumetanide (Bumex)
   Canrenone (Aldadiene, Aldactone [Germany], Phanurane
      [France], Soldactone [Switzerland])
   Chlormerodrin (Orimercur [Spain])
   Chlortalidone (Hygroton, Hylidone, Thalitone)
   Diclofenamide (Daranide, Oratrol, Fenamide)
   Ethacrynic Acid (Edecrin)
   Furosemide (Lasix Hydrochlorothiazide, Esidrix, Hydro-
      Diuril, Oretic, Thiuretic)
   Mannitol (IV only) (Osmitol)
   Mersalyl (Salyrgan)
   Spironolactone (Alatone, Aldactone)
   Torsemide (Demadex)
   Triamterene-related substances (Dyrenium, Dyazide)

## APPETITE SUPPRESSANTS

The desire to eat comes from a balance of brain signals. Stomach emptiness, low blood sugar, or the sight and smell of tasty food can trigger hunger centers in the brain that initiate eating. Stomach fullness, the presence of fat and sugar in the bloodstream, and other signals trigger satiety—the natural suppression of appetite after eating. Different centers in the brain control these two processes. Theoretically, using drugs to control appetite is just a matter of shutting down the hunger center, or artificially stimulating the satiety center.

All the appetite suppressants on the market inhibit the hunger center, stimulate the satiety center, or do both. Each of the stimulants described in Chapter 6 decrease appetite by affecting the hunger center. This makes sense because stimulants trigger the "flight or fight" response. If you are getting ready to flee or to fight, it is *not* the time to be eating.

How well do appetite suppressants work? Many studies have shown that they can increase weight loss a pound or two a week for up to a month. But diet drugs don't work forever because tolerance builds up after a few weeks. So they can help someone trying to lose five to ten pounds, but they aren't much use for someone who needs to lose a lot more.

**Drugs Marketed as Appetite Suppressants in the United States**

| Drug name | Brand name |
|---|---|
| Phentermine | Adipex,. Fastin, Bontril |
| Methamphetamine | Desoxyn |
| Phendimetrazine | Prelu-2 |

Sibutramine                    Meridia

Phenylpropanolamine            Dexatrim

These drugs also come with some big drawbacks. They all have major side effects that come from increasing the levels of neurochemicals in the brain. Every one of the drugs functions by stimulating the actions of dopamine, norepinephrine, serotonin, or some combination of the three (see Chapter 6). Drugs that increase dopamine are potentially addicting, and they are rarely recommended for appetite suppression because of the high risk of abuse. Norepinephrine is the neurotransmitter of the sympathetic nervous system (Chapter 6), and if present at higher-than-natural levels it overstimulates heart rate and raises blood pressure.

In the potentially hugely profitable search for a drug that can suppress appetite without adverse effects, scientists and marketers had high hopes for the combination of a drug that releases dopamine (like phentermine) with a nonaddictive drug that releases serotonin (like fenfluramine). The result was the popular diet drug combination fen-phen, which acts by both suppressing the hunger center and stimulating the satiety center. But it turned out that in some people fen-phen causes a rare but usually fatal disease called *primary pulmonary hypertension*. A number of fen-phen users in Europe died. Other users suffered damage to the valves between the two chambers of the heart. In response, the makers of fen-phen withdrew the drug from the market.

A drug company has just released a new drug called sibutramine (Meridia) that acts by increasing both norepinephrine and serotonin. Sibutramine can increase heart rate and blood pressure in some people by mimicking the effects of norepinephrine on the heart, but these effects seem to be mild. So far, sibutramine has shown no tendency to cause the same sorts of trouble caused by fenfluramine, so it may offer some real advantages to obese dieters. However, it is potentially riskier for an athlete in training because it stimulates the heart more.

What are the risks of stimulant appetite suppressants for the healthy, fit athlete? Any human being, athletic or not, can become addicted to amphetamine. All the stimulants, including amphetamine, sibutramine, and ephedrine, increase the risk of dangerously irregular heartbeats during maximal exercise. Taking such drugs during training is especially dangerous for obese people, whose cardiovascular system is already stressed by the excess body weight they carry. Only when taken according to directions from a physician, and not under competition or training conditions, can the appetite suppressants listed above be safe and effective.

## Purging and Vomiting

Certain sports impose extreme limits on body weight. Some athletes cope by self-induced vomiting after meals and purging with laxatives, strategies they have in common with people who suffer from anorexia nervosa or bulimia nervosa. Yet athletes may be less likely to recognize these behaviors as severely dysfunctional, which they are. They are also self-defeating if one's goal is good health and optimizing physical performance.

Vomiting can cause a loss of electrolytes (sodium and potassium) that are normally absorbed after a meal. This can eventually lead to disturbances of heart rhythm and other bodily functions. Vomiting also exposes the esophagus and mouth to corrosive stomach acid, which should never be there. Daily vomiting damages these sensitive tissues and can even damage tooth enamel. Ipecac, the most common drug used to induce vomiting, is given as a one-time treatment in emergency rooms for accidental poisonings. If you take it daily it can damage the heart. This practice may have led to the death of Karen Carpenter, a popular singer in the 1970s

Purging with laxatives makes even less sense. You temporarily lose weight because you flush out the lower intestines and some bodily water, as well. The problem is that all the calories have been absorbed from the food by the time it gets to the lower intestine, and flushing it out at this point only gets rid of waste and water. The loss of water is a problem because you can easily become dehydrated, especially when you're training. Finally, you can become so dependent on laxatives that you can't have a regular bowel movement without them.

## *"Fat-Burning" Drugs*

If you think that fat-burning drugs are the magic bullet that will cause fat to melt away with no effort, think again. The idea behind "fat-burning" drugs is to increase energy use without exercise. In theory it's a good idea since so much energy is used at rest, and even a modest rise in the rate of resting metabolism would burn a lot of calories. Unfortunately, the only drugs that work are very dangerous.

### THYROID HORMONE, OR TRIIODOTHYRONINE

Thyroid hormone is released by the thyroid gland in the neck. It regulates the rate of basal metabolism in the body. People with low thyroid hormone levels gain weight easily and tend to be tired, depressed, and cold. People with high levels are energetic and very lean since their bodies burn more energy. Some athletes have tried to lose weight by taking thyroid hormone pills to speed up their metabolism.

So what's the harm? Thyroid hormone increases the actions of the sympathetic nervous system, and at higher than normal levels it can cause dangerous increases in heart rate and blood pressure. It also raises your body temperature, and this causes every enzyme in your body to work faster than normal. In patients with thyroid disease, levels of thyroid hormone that cause elevated body temperature and increased heart rate can be fatal. Finally, thyroid hormone forces the body to use protein for fuel, and no athlete wants to use up the muscle protein she has worked so hard to build up.

## DNP (DINITROPHENOL)

Body builders use dinitrophenol (DNP) for "fat stripping." Like thyroid hormone, DNP increases the resting rate of metabolism and body temperature—an effect that has been known for over one hundred years. It can cause an extremely rapid loss of body fat. Sounds like a miracle drug, right? Actually, DNP is extremely dangerous. Doses 70 percent above the "effective" dose can kill you.

DNP was first used to help people lose weight in the late 1800s. Physicians of the time gave it in carefully regulated doses, but it soon became included in unregulated patent medicines. The first clue about the dangers of DNP was that it caused cataracts in some people. It also caused numerous poisonings and even deaths. Eventually public outcry about its dangers grew, and the FDA banned it.

DNP interferes with energy metabolism at the cellular level. In essence, it causes the energy-generating machinery in the cell to just whir away, generating heat but not producing energy. The cell uses up energy instead of making it. If there is too much DNP in the body, eventually all the body's energy is used up, and you die.

These days DNP is widely touted on the Internet, especially by body builders who take dangerous doses. In the search for an ideal appearance, they risk death or serious health problems.

## EPHEDRINE AND OTHER STIMULANTS

Stimulants work to burn fat, but not very well. They stimulate the burning of *brown fat,* which is a special kind of fat that is found more in babies than in adults. Brown fat actually produces heat instead of providing glucose. This serves a useful purpose in infants, who burn it to keep warm. Stimulants like ephedrine activate this process, causing a slight increase in heat production and thus energy consumption. They would stimulate brown fat and burn calories well in babies but not much in adults because we don't have much brown fat.

The hormone norepinephrine is active in the sympathetic nervous system and promotes the breakdown of fat (see Chapter 6). All drugs that mimic the action of norepinephrine can break down fat, but that isn't enough to cause weight loss. These drugs don't burn energy, they just make fat available as a fuel—which is like providing firewood but no fire. There is just no getting around the fact that you have to exercise to burn calories safely.

## CAFFEINE AND THEOPHYLLINE

Another weight-loss strategy takes advantage of the fact that some hormones in our bodies prevent fat breakdown, and others cause the body to store fat after a meal. One of these hormones is adenosine, and its actions are blocked by caffeine and theo-phylline (a stimulant found in tea). Drugs that block the action of adenosine have long been marketed as diet aids in a variety of preparations. Many diet pills contain caffeine because its stimu-lant actions raise the basal metabolic rate, and it also minimally inhibits the body's ability to store fat.

Now there are "fat-melting" creams containing theophylline. The idea of rubbing a cream on the skin to melt fat is very appeal-ing, and thighs are a popular target. Unlike caffeine, theophylline passes through cells very well and can enter the fat below. Does it work? Most of the research on the topic is poor, so it remains an open question. A couple of studies have reported that thigh cir-cumference was decreased by regular application of theophylline cream, but they did not determine where the fat went or if body weight decreased. It is unlikely that breaking down fat in a spe-cific area like the thighs would change anyone's body weight. Most likely, if there really were a decrease in the amount of fat on the thighs, the fatty acids were simply redeposited somewhere else.

## "Fat-Blocking" Drugs

Of course, there is one other choice in the fat wars: never absorb calories in the first place. This was actually the theme of a short story by Kurt Vonnegut years ago, and now it has become med-ical reality. The new drug Orlistat prevents some amount of fat absorption by the intestine. This seems like a really ingenious idea. You get to eat whatever you want and not absorb the calo-ries. Unfortunately, the reality is somewhat less appealing. The biggest problem with this drug is where the fat goes: out the other end. Fat that is not absorbed is eliminated in the feces, and lots of fat in the feces causes diarrhea. Too, it provides extra nutrients for gut bacteria, which metabolize more actively and create gas. So diarrhea and flatulence are significant enough side effects to limit how much of this drug you can tolerate. Too, people on this drug won't absorb fat-soluble vitamins, so they need to be sure to take adequate vitamin supplements. In the end, clinical studies show that people taking this drug tend to lose 10 to 20 pounds, and they also tend to gain the weight right back when they stop.

## Special Issues for Women

Women athletes face special risks when they lose too much weight. Intensive training coupled with not eating enough can reduce weight so much that their menstrual periods stop. This can be a major problem because when women stop having menstrual cycles (either during intensive training, or after menopause), they no longer produce enough estrogen to keep their calcium levels high enough for strong bones. Bones with too little calcium are more likely to fracture —including stress fractures from the impact of training. Once a bone is weakened in this way, it is very difficult to get it back to its previous strength. Estrogen also keeps cholesterol levels in check, and women who are deficient in estrogen have an increased risk of heart attacks. If a woman stops having her period, she should talk to a physician. In some cases an oral contraceptive might be recommended to maintain healthy amounts of estrogen.

## Putting It All Together: Burn Fat with Ephedrine and Caffeine?

Many nutritional supplements now include ephedrine or caffeine, citing research in obese patients showing weight loss during this treatment. This makes sense because caffeine activates the breakdown of fats, and ephedrine releases norepinephrine, which activates fat breakdown and increases energy use. Ephedrine can also decrease appetite by acting on the brain. What the advertisements don't say is that the weight loss is quite modest—typically 10 pounds over several months.

If these drugs are so powerful, why is the weight loss so small? Because they cause bad side effects that limit the amounts that people can take. Neither ephedrine nor caffeine works only on fat. Ephedrine can stimulate the whole sympathetic nervous system, dangerously increasing blood pressure and heart rate. It can lead to heart attacks and strokes even in young people. Healthy young athletes have died from excessive use of ephedrine for performance enhancement. High levels of caffeine can produce insomnia, even seizures.

Finally, athletes stand to gain little from these drugs because their training levels are generally high enough to lose weight without having to eat less. Even in the absence of intensive training, these drugs are marginally effective at best—and often dangerous.

## *The Bottom Line*

1. You can lose weight by eating less, by exercising more, or by doing both—which works best.
2. Long-term or repeated dieting slows metabolism, making it harder to decrease weight just by restricting food.
3. Trying to lose pounds with diuretics or cathartics is dangerous and doesn't work. All you lose is water, which comes right back.
4. Appetite suppressants can be helpful if the amount of weight you want to lose is in the range of 10 to 20 pounds.
5. Dinitrophenol and thyroid hormone increase metabolic rate, but they are extremely dangerous.
6. Ephedrine and caffeine combinations may slightly increase energy consumption, but they also stimulate the sympathetic nervous system and can have dangerous effects on the heart.

Chapter 5

# BUILDING MUSCLE MASS
# AND STRENGTH

## CONTENTS

Anabolic Steroids
  *Normal Effects of Testosterone-like Hormones*
The Use of Anabolic Steroids in Sports
Who Takes Steroids Now?
How Anabolic Steroids Increase Muscle Size
The Dangerous Side Effects of Anabolic Steroids
  *Special Risks for Women*
  *Special Risks for Adolescents*
  *Risks to the Reproductive System of Men*
  *The Heart and Circulatory System*
  *What about Cancer?*
  *Liver Disease*
  *"'Roid Rage" and Other Psychological Effects*
'Roid Rage: Abstracted from Steroid Nightmare by Kirk
  *Vinchattle*
continued on next page

*Are Steroids Addictive?*

**Various Steroid Preparations**

*What Does a Human Pregnancy Test Have in Common*
*with Anabolic Steroids?*

**Androstenedione and DHEA: Natural and Safe**
**Steroids?**

**Growth Hormone and Its Friends**

*IGF (Somatomedin)*

*GHB and Other Growth Hormone Releasing Agents*

GROWTH HORMONE THE NATURAL WAY: GET A GOOD
NIGHT'S SLEEP

**Clenbuterol**

**Creatine Phosphate**

**Insulin and Oral Hypoglycemic Drugs**

**Chromium Piccolinate**

**Amino Acid Supplements**

*Sources of Amino Acids*

*How Much Protein?*

*Dieting Before Weight-Lifting Competitions:*
*Amino Acids and Energy*

**Specific Amino Acids**

**The Bottom Line**

Athletes want drugs that they can take during training to increase muscle mass and strength, and they prefer drugs that are either legal or undetectable at the time of performance (or testing). The drugs listed in this chapter are all used for this purpose. Some of them do work, but any drug that is effective is (1) probably dangerous to the user and (2) illegal in most competitive environments. Anabolic drugs increase production of protein in the muscle. Some act as natural hormones to stimulate protein synthesis (the making of proteins). These include anabolic steroids, growth hormone, and insulin. Others like clenbuterol and GHB allegedly stimulate the body to produce more of these hormones on its own. Finally, nutritional supplements that are supposed to provide more amino acids, the building blocks of protein, are widely touted as safe, natural ways to augment muscle growth. Recently, a flood of trace nutrients have joined the amino acids as nutritional supplements to increase muscle mass.

## Anabolic Steroids

Anabolic steroids were probably the first drugs that athletes of the modern era used to enhance athletic performance. *Anabolic steroids* are natural hormones produced by the body that help build muscle. The male sex hormone testosterone is the most active anabolic steroid in the human body. Cortisol, the stress hormone produced by the adrenal gland, is also a steroid, but it is a *catabolic steroid* that tears muscle down. Steroid hormones used to treat asthma are variations of cortisol, and these have no anabolic effects, so you don't have to worry that you are taking banned steroids if you are just treating your asthma. In fact, the high doses of these catabolic steroids that are used to treat autoimmune diseases produce muscle loss as a severe side effect.

Men have bigger muscles than women because their bodies produce much more of the male hormone testosterone. When boys go through puberty, their testicles produce more testosterone, which triggers the rapid increase in height and muscle mass that boys experience. Testosterone treatment can help boys with underdeveloped testicles go through normal puberty. The idea that testosterone could increase muscle mass in athletes was a natural extension of our knowledge of how normal male bodies develop.

Anabolic steroids affect more than muscle mass. The term *anabolic* is really a bit of a misnomer because testosterone mainly facilitates reproduction. Testosterone is an important part of sperm production and helps to create secondary sexual characteristics in men, including male-pattern facial, chest, and limb hair, male-pattern baldness, male-type body odor, and increased sweating. You may remember the adage of a bygone era that men sweat but women perspire. Testosterone, not ladylike behavior, is what's responsible for the larger number of sweat glands and greater volume of sweat that men produce. Testosterone increases the size of the larynx, leading to the deeper voice of adult men, and creates more red blood cells. Testosterone also changes the pattern of blood lipids to one that is more likely to lead to the development of cardiovascular disease. Given all of these natural effects of testosterone, it's not surprising that there is no such thing as a purely "anabolic" steroid that can stimulate muscle growth without causing all the other effects of testosterone. These other effects contribute to many of the dangerous consequences of anabolic steroid use in sports.

The "good" effects of anabolic steroids cannot be separated from the "bad" effects of testosterone because testosterone receptors that build muscles are exactly like the receptors that enlarge the larynx or cause hair loss. Therefore, any drug that works in the muscle also works elsewhere in the body.

## NORMAL EFFECTS OF TESTOSTERONE-LIKE HORMONES

*Puberty:* sexual development, increase in height, muscle deposition, hair development, deepening of voice

*Reproduction:* libido, sperm production

*Circulation:* red blood cell formation, clotting factors, blood volume

## The Use of Anabolic Steroids in Sports

Russian weight lifters in the 1954 world weight lifting competition introduced anabolic steroids to international athletic competition. This practice was widely adopted, including by American coaches, and by the 1964 Olympics, the practice was widespread. The East German women's swim teams of the 1960s through the 1980s dominated the sport—and for good reason. They received injections of testosterone throughout their training. Women's bodies normally produce only a tiny amount of testosterone. The huge increase in testosterone these women received let them develop muscles much bigger than women typically can, even during intensive weight training. Upper-body muscle mass generally translates into improved swimming times, and these women showed dramatically improved performance. The Chinese women's swim team in the Los Angeles Olympics tried the same strategy. Again, their upper body mass increased, and swimming times decreased. Unfortunately, they misjudged the greatly improved sensitivity of the testing technique. Steroids were detected in a number of these athletes, and they were disqualified.

The benefit of anabolic steroids to women athletes is clear because even small amounts of testosterone are way above the typical levels for women. But what about normal men who have already gone through puberty? Science took us a step backward here. For years, scientists stated that carefully conducted laboratory research could not show that anabolic steroids cause any improvement of performance in normal men. At the same time, weight lifters and other athletes were touting their benefits. Both the scientists and weight lifters were right. Under normal circumstances, men produce so much testosterone that even doubling or tripling testosterone levels really doesn't help. This is exactly what the "careful scientific studies" did. Furthermore, they put the subjects on an exercise regimen at the same time. All the men deposited more muscle because they were exercising, and the steroids didn't add much. On the other hand, athletes don't take normal doses, and they are not looking for "statistically significant" effects. They often take huge doses, and a 1 percent improvement in performance can mean the difference between winning and losing. Huge doses of testosterone can increase muscle mass, as weight lifters have claimed for years.

## Who Takes Steroids Now?

Use of anabolic steroids began with elite competitive athletes, but today it includes even high school students who are taking anabolic steroids for cosmetic purposes. Most researchers estimate that 3 to 5 percent of high school age athletes and 5 to 15 percent of adult athletes use performance-enhancing drugs (mainly anabolic steroids). The level of anabolic steroid use among young athletes exceeds use of any drugs other than alcohol, nicotine, or marijuana. Ironically, the introduction of testing has drastically reduced the incidence of anabolic steroid use in international elite competitions, although it still happens. Exact numbers are hard to come by because these athletes have also become better and better at escaping the detection, but they are clearly a small number (1 to 2 percent by some estimates).

## How Anabolic Steroids Increase Muscle Size

Anabolic steroids do increase the size of muscle fibers. They do this by entering muscle cells and stimulating the production of proteins. However, strength increases less than muscle size because testosterone can cause fluid retention, which swells the muscles without making them stronger. For body builders this doesn't matter—as long as they are bigger, actual strength doesn't matter.

How well does increased muscle size translate to increased performance after anabolic steroid use? The jury is still out on this. The American College of Sports Medicine has stated that anabolic steroids can increase body mass, but they do not increase aerobic power or capacity for muscular exercise. In the end, we have to remember that research in this area is extremely controversial, and slight performance benefits in some situations mean the differences between winning and losing.

One mystery surrounding the claims that anabolic steroids increase muscle size is that the normal male body produces about as much testosterone as it can use. Doubling or tripling levels really shouldn't accomplish anything, and it doesn't. It takes amounts from ten to one hundred times normal values to get results. The hormone cortisol that breaks muscle down enters the picture here. Cortisol and testosterone are pretty similar to each other chemically. When tremendous excesses of testosterone are present, testosterone can actually bind to the cortisol receptors and keep cortisol from doing its normal job of breaking down protein. In this way, anabolic steroids may increase muscle mass in part by preventing the normal muscle breakdown by another hormone.

## The Dangerous Side Effects of Anabolic Steroids

The huge amounts of anabolic steroids that athletes must take to get some benefit in muscle size present some very real risks to users. The first risk is simple to understand. Anabolic steroid use increases strains and tears of the tendons and ligaments connected to the muscle. These tissues are not as elastic as muscle, and it's possible that they just can't keep up with the abrupt increase in muscle size that the anabolic steroids cause. Up to 65 percent of the East German athletes who were given anabolic steroids during training experienced tightness or some other tendon/ligament problem.

Anabolic steroids can also change the profile of fats in the blood to a pattern that increases the risk of cardiovascular disease, and they can decrease sperm production and cause impotence. Finally, a growing number of individual cases indicate that direct damage to the heart muscle occurs in some users.

## SPECIAL RISKS FOR WOMEN

Young women face special risks from anabolic steroid use because even small doses cause tremendous increases in their testosterone levels. Women's bodies have testosterone receptors, and they respond to the hormone if it is there. Naturally they make only about 5 percent of what men produce. Increasing that amount to levels comparable to normal males causes irreversible changes. The clitoris enlarges, as does the larynx, leading to a permanent deepening of the voice. Male-pattern baldness may also develop, other body hair coarsens, and some women develop bad acne. While these changes are mainly cosmetic, more dangerous changes also occur, such as the change in pattern of blood lipids that increases risk of cardiovascular disease. Women who use anabolic steroids lose the normal protection their gender provides against cardiovascular disease. Anabolic steroids also inhibit menstrual cycles and can lower libido (or increase it if the athlete just uses small doses).

## SPECIAL RISKS FOR ADOLESCENTS

Teenagers of either gender who have not finished growing face an additional risk if they take anabolic steroids. The rapid rise in testosterone in boys during puberty stimulates bone growth and so increases height, but it also will make bones stop growing. Testosterone both stimulates the normal rapid bone growth during puberty and, when it is done, triggers the end of this process. When teenage athletes take large doses of anabolic steroids, they can end up shorter than they would have been if they hadn't used anabolic steroids. We don't know yet what such large doses of anabolic steroids do to the reproductive system during puberty. This uncertainty is particularly troubling because so many high school students take these drugs.

## RISKS TO THE REPRODUCTIVE SYSTEM OF MEN

Normal adult men who take anabolic steroids don't suffer the irreversible effects described for women and adolescents. Nevertheless, there are bad health consequences. Effects on the reproductive system depend on how much the athlete takes. With small doses, libido may increase. High doses of anabolic steroids do the opposite: they "trick" the body into thinking that it is producing too much male hormone, and so the testes stop making testosterone and sperm, and the testes actually atrophy (shrink). These effects gradually reverse when steroid use is stopped. A certain percentage of each dose of certain anabolic steroids (testosterone itself and some of its precursors like androstenedione ["andro"]) is converted in the body to the female sex hormone estradiol. This can lead to the development of breast tissue—usually a pretty unpopular side effect.

## THE HEART AND CIRCULATORY SYSTEM

High doses of anabolic steroids can enlarge the heart, thickening its walls to the point that the heart can't pump efficiently. This effect can reverse slowly after the athlete stops using steroids, but sometimes it doesn't.

Many cases of heart attacks in anabolic steroid users have also been reported. There are probably several reasons for this. Anabolic steroids decrease the levels of protective high density lipoproteins (HDL—"good cholesterol") and increase the low density lipoproteins (LDL—the "bad cholesterol") that increase risk of heart attacks. The normal effects of testosterone may be one reason that men are more vulnerable to heart attacks than premenopausal women. Estrogen and the absence of testosterone lead to a pattern of blood lipids that is higher in HDL and lower in LDL. Finally, anabolic steroids also increase the stickiness of blood cells called *platelets*. This clumping is one of the first steps in the formation of dangerous plaques inside blood vessels. Anabolic steroids increase the number of red blood cells, increase the factors in the blood that produce blood clots, and can increase blood pressure by causing fluid retention. Overall, they can place a big strain on the cardiovascular system.

## WHAT ABOUT CANCER?

Despite several high-profile cases like that of football player Lyle Alzedo, liver and brain cancer are not big concerns with anabolic steroids, but cancer of the reproductive organs *is* a concern. The reproductive organs are the most sensitive to testosterone-like hormones, and elevated levels of anabolic steroids may be a factor in the development of prostate and testicular cancer. Unfortunately, it's hard to know for sure if a treatment like anabolic steroids causes cancers that appear years after use. Sometimes it's just not possible to know what got the cancer-promoting process started.

## LIVER DISEASE

All the anabolic steroids that can be taken in pill form can cause several different liver diseases. These drugs most often cause a benign type of liver tumor that might go away when steroid use is stopped. However, occasionally these tumors are malignant and fatal. Anabolic steroids also sometimes cause a condition called *peliosis hepatitis*, a condition in which normal liver tissue is replaced with blood-filled cysts. Sometimes these rupture and can cause a fatal hemorrhage.

## "'ROID RAGE" AND OTHER PSYCHOLOGICAL EFFECTS

No steroid effect has gained more press than the much-touted "'roid rage"—bouts of reportedly uncontrollable hostility and aggression that are said to be triggered by high doses of anabolic steroids. 'Roid rage has been blamed for many incidents of domestic violence associated with professional athletes in the last ten years. But is it real?

The idea that testosterone increases aggression came from some highly publicized studies that reported high testosterone levels in violent prison inmates compared to nonviolent inmates. These findings are controversial, as not every study has gotten such clear-cut findings. The association between aggression and testosterone is even weaker in men and women in the general population. On the other hand, numerous case reports have documented excessive aggression in athletes who are taking large doses of anabolic steroids. Research in animals tells a similar

story. Showing that testosterone causes aggression in normal animals is difficult, but extreme excesses or deficiencies of testosterone do seem to influence aggression. For example, laboratory
animals become less aggressive when their testes are removed,
and aggression returns when the lost testosterone is restored. So
even though the scientific literature does not provide a definitive
answer to the question of whether anabolic steroids promote
aggressiveness, it is reasonable to take seriously the self-reports of
athletes who often note increased irritability and hostility.

Anabolic steroids have other psychological effects that are
better documented. They can cause an increased sense of well-
being, and at toxically high doses this can become *hypomania*—an
elevation of mood and a need to be active that is pathological.
Users like this state because they feel more energetic and happier.

## 'Roid Rage
### Abstracted from *Steroid Nightmare*
### by Kirk Vinchattle

I always felt, when I was on steroids, that something wasn't
quite right. I'm calm, always calm. But, the littlest things
would tick me off. When I'd get behind an old lady, who
was going slow on the highway, I'd become irate, to say the
least. I felt like screaming. . . . I was cussing and pounding
my fist. I never went uncontrollable, but the worst thing
was my friend was also on steroids. We'd get close to slug-
ging it out in some arguments, before we were calm. We
were always on edge, ready to snap. You always feel aggressive, superior, invincible.

The problem is that hypomanic people don't always make good or safe decisions, and in some cases this can cross over into an overtly psychotic, manic state. Furthermore, abrupt withdrawal of steroids can trigger a depressive episode.

## ARE STEROIDS ADDICTIVE?

Are anabolic steroids really addictive, in the way that cocaine and heroin are? There certainly has been a lot of media interest in this question, and the National Institute of Drug Abuse (NIDA) and the Drug Enforcement Agency (DEA) have classified them in this way. Scientifically, we don't really know whether this is true or not. Addictive drugs stimulate the "reward" system in the brain, and most scientists think that biochemical changes in the brain contribute to the compulsive pattern of drug taking that we describe as addiction. Steroids don't stimulate the reward system; however, steroid users clearly use compulsively, despite negative consequences. When a drug user loses control over use, and uses drugs despite the negative consequences, he has a problem, regardless of whether we would measure "addictive" changes in brain chemistry or not. Furthermore, steroid users often experience mood disorders or even depression that could be described as withdrawal when they stop. (However, from that perspective, pregnancy could be viewed as addictive, since an abrupt change in mood is associated with the equally huge endocrine changes at the end of pregnancy.) We are reluctant to describe anabolic steroids as addictive, but steroid use certainly has bad health consequences. And people certainly keep using steroids even though they understand these consequences, often because they are afraid of losing all the muscle mass that has been gained. So even if anabolic steroids don't stimulate the reward system in the way of drugs classically understood to be "addictive," people do use them in a compulsive and health-damaging way to avoid the reversal of their effects.

*Major Dangerous Anabolic Side Effects in Adults*
   Increased vulnerability to damage to tendons and cartilage
   Increased risk of cardiovascular disease: cardiac hypertrophy, altered blood lipids
   Increased fluid retention, blood pressure
   Increase or decrease in libido, decreased reproductive function
   Irritability, mania
   Reproductive tract cancer

## Various Steroid Preparations

There are many different anabolic steroid preparations. All of them are both *anabolic* (muscle building) and *androgenic* (masculinizing). They differ from each other in several ways: (1) how they are given (by injection or in pill form), (2) how long they stay in the body, and (3) the tendency to be converted to the female sex hormone estradiol and so cause breast development and other feminizing qualities.

Testosterone must be injected because the liver degrades it so quickly that pill forms are not effective. If the molecule is changed slightly, it can be effective in pill form because it isn't so degraded by the liver. Unfortunately, this change also causes liver damage.

Many athletes are very sophisticated in their choice of anabolic steroids. One major goal of some athletes is to use drugs that tests can't detect. To achieve this goal, athletes often take long-lasting oral preparations during the early phases of training, then switch to testosterone itself before major competitions to allow the other compounds to disappear. The liver eliminates testosterone itself quickly, and once levels fall to near normal, tests can't tell the difference between testosterone produced by the testes and testosterone provided by pills.

Dose regimens that athletes use are often staggeringly high in conventional medical terms. Athletes often take anabolic steroids in "pyramids" of gradually increasing and then decreasing doses. They "stack," or combine, drugs and take doses that are often at least one hundred times greater than those needed to produce normal levels of testosterone. For example, one published regimen involves taking an oral anabolic steroid every day, adding testosterone injections every five days for about eight weeks. Then as the doses are decreased, human chorionic gonadotropin (hCG) or something similar is begun to allow the testes to start again. These regimens are repeated in "cycles" with breaks in between.

When athletes want to avoid the feminizing side effects of anabolic steroids like testosterone, they sometimes take drugs that block the actions of estrogen (like Tamoxifen) or drugs that prevent the conversion of testosterone to estrogen (like Testolactone [Teslac]). There are also drugs that can stimulate the atrophied testes to start producing sperm and testosterone again. Some athletes use these drugs to jump start their own systems after they stop an anabolic steroid "pyramid." Clearly this kind of drug use, and counteruse, can create a complicated set of effects. Since most people that end up going down this road do so without adequate medical supervision, the results can be dangerous.

The lists below show some common drugs in this category, including some of the brand names they're sold under. This is only a partial list of all possible anabolic steroids, and most European drugs are omitted.

*Anabolic Steroids*
**Taken by Injection**
Testosterone (Malogen, Malogex, Delatestryl, Testoject)
Testosterone cypionate (Depo-testosterone, Textex)
Testosterone enanthate (Delatestryl)
Nandrolone (Deca-Durabolin, Durabolin, Kabolin, Nandrobolic)

**Taken by Mouth (Tendency for Liver Problems)**
Oxandrololone (Anavar)
Oxymetholone (Anadrol, Anapolon 50, Androyd)
Fluoxymesterone (Halotestin, Ora-Testryl, Ultradren)
Methyltestosterone (Android, Estratest, Testred, Virilon)

*Steroids That Can Be Converted to Estradiol and Cause Breast Development*
Oxymetholone (Anadrol, Anapolon 50, Adroyd)
Testosterone (Malogen, Malogex, Delatestryl, Testoject)
Testosterone cypionate (Depo-testosterone, Textex)
Testosterone enanthate (Delatestryl)

*Veterinary Steroids (Steroids Approved for Use in Animals)*
Boldenone (Equipoise)
Trenbolone acetate (Finaplix)
Stanozolol (Winstrol, Stromba)

*Drugs Not Approved for Marketing in the United States*
  Bolasterone (Vebonol)
  Clostebol (Steranobol)
  Dehydrochlormethyl-testosterone (Turinabol)
  Dihydrotestosterone (Stanolone)
  Mesterolone (Androviron, Proviron)—oral
  Metandienone (Danabol, Dianabol)
  Methenolone (Primobolan, Primonabol-Depot)—oral testos-
    terone ester, not toxic to liver
  Methandrostenolone (Dianabol)—oral
  Norethandrolone (Nilevar)

## WHAT DOES A HUMAN PREGNANCY TEST HAVE IN COMMON WITH ANABOLIC STEROIDS?

Human chorionic gonadotropin (hCG) is a hormone normally produced by the body early in pregnancy that helps the embryo to survive in the uterus. It is the hormone measured with early-pregnancy kits. Some male athletes take injections of this pregnancy hormone to increase the ability of their body to produce testosterone and to prevent the atrophy of the testicles that results from taking large doses of anabolic steroids. This is often done at the end of a "stacking" regimen in order to get the athlete's own testosterone production started again. If these male athletes were to take an early pregnancy test, they would appear to be pregnant! Another drug, gonadotropin releasing hormone (gonadorelin, or FACTREL), accomplishes the same thing. This molecule stimulates the release of luteinizing hormone and follicle-stimulating hormone from the pituitary gland. They can stimulate the testicles just like hCG.

## Androstenedione and DHEA: Natural and Safe Steroids?

Mark McGuire set a new season-home-run record for baseball in 1998, and at the same time became the poster boy for "andro," the "natural and safe" steroid. Although andro is banned by the USOC and a number of other sporting groups, it isn't banned by baseball, and his use of this product caused a rush of enthusiastic use by amateur athletes. What is the truth about this miracle steroid?

Androstenedione is a steroid that the adrenal glands normally produce in minute amounts. It plays a very small role in the production of testosterone—about 5 percent of androstenedione is turned into testosterone. Since it *is* a natural product, it has been touted as a "safe" anabolic steroid. Yet several old scientific studies, as well as a recent study sparked by current interest in andro, have shown that the amounts that athletes typically use at best marginally increase testosterone levels and don't measurably improve strength. However, early studies with testosterone had similarly unimpressive results, and it is possible that heroic doses might increase testosterone a little, perhaps enough for an increase in strength in certain individuals.

Despite its possible benefits to training, andro has another drawback. It's converted into estrogen at a higher rate than it's turned into testosterone. A recent study showed that while daily andro use didn't increase testosterone particularly, it did increase the female hormone estradiol.

DHEA (dihydroepiandrosterone), like andro, is a precursor (a building block) for testosterone. In fact, it's converted into andro, then eventually into testosterone. Physicians who treat the elderly have been interested in DHEA for years, ever since it was observed that DHEA levels gradually fall during aging. Clinical studies that tried to halt aging by supplementing falling DHEA levels obviously met with limited success, but high doses of DHEA did improve lean body mass in the elderly. As with andro, this required very high doses, and women who took DHEA experienced the same masculinizing effects as female athletes who take anabolic steroids.

Many similar steroidlike compounds are sold as supplements, including 19-norandrostenedione, 19-norandrostenediol, and 5-androstenediol. The current marketing strategy is to call them "pro-hormones" that should be converted to testosterone in the body. Some of these steroid derivatives block the actions of the stress hormone cortisol and have been tested experimentally in the hopes that they could decrease cortisol-mediated inflammation. However, we just don't know much about them yet. We do know that anabolic steroid tests used for athletes detect some of these compounds, because several high-profile athletes were disqualified after international meets following use of these pro-hormones.

Finally, there are other preparations out there that are intended to provide anabolic action, with attractive names like "testicular powder." Advertisers provide no information about these powders—probably ground up animal testicles—which are supposed to have testosterone in them. It's not clear what is in these drugs, or how much. The best hope is that they do nothing.

## Growth Hormone and Its Friends

Growth hormone is produced by the pituitary gland and causes rapid skeletal growth and height increase during puberty. In adults, it has slight but measurable effects on muscle deposition and cartilage growth, and it also contributes to the control of blood-sugar levels. The fact that growth hormone is "natural," lasts only a short time in the body, and is virtually impossible to detect with current testing methods has led to its increased use.

Until 1985, human cadavers were the only available source of growth hormone. It was extremely rare, and potentially contaminated with a virus that could cause Creutzfeldt-Jakob disease, a devastating disease that causes progressive destruction of the brain. Biotechnology eliminated this risk, making laboratory-produced growth hormone widely available. This was a godsend to the children who truly needed treatment, but it also encouraged misuse of growth hormone, both by physicians willing to respond to anxious patients and by athletes.

Growth hormone doesn't work on bone itself. It goes to the liver and causes the production of growth factors that stimulate bone growth. The hormone is degraded within minutes in the blood, but the growth factors produced by the liver last some hours. Growth hormone is virtually impossible to detect in blood if more than a couple of days pass between use and testing, making it tempting to use for purposes of performance enhancement.

Does growth hormone really work? There is much less research available on growth hormone than on anabolic steroids because its use for performance enhancement is relatively new. Growth hormone can definitely improve lean body mass in people who don't have enough growth hormone, like the elderly, and those who can't make enough growth hormone on their own. But its effects on normal, healthy people with enough growth hormone are very small at best. It does cause cartilage to grow, which athletes like because it may compensate for the cartilage and tendon problems associated with anabolic steroid use. However, as usual, studies that used safe doses of the drug may not predict what happens with use of the near-toxic doses that athletes often take to get a performance-enhancing effect.

There are some definite downsides to using growth hormone. It can cause organs like the liver and spleen to enlarge. In fact, many body builders say that they can recognize someone who is using growth hormone because liver growth obscures the abdominal muscle, ruining the "six pack" look. In adults bone growth occurs in the chin and other bones of the face, and this can make users look very strange. Everyone has seen pictures of "giants" who suffer from a disease called *acromegaly*, which results from too much growth hormone. These people are not just extra tall. Their faces are distorted, with large chins, noses, ears, and tongues, a stubby appearance of the fingers and toes, and coarsening of skin and body hair.

Growth hormone consequences are not just cosmetic. Growth hormone helps to control blood glucose, and its use can lead to symptoms of diabetes. Finally, since taking growth hormone requires injections, there are always such significant risks as transmission of HIV and other infectious diseases.

## Forms of Growth Hormone

Protropin (made in bacteria)
Humatrope (made in bacteria)
Crescormon (human cadavar)
Assellacrin (human cadavar)
(*The latter two are marketed in Europe and are illegal in the United States because of the possibility of Creutzfeld-Jacob disease.*)

## Side Effects of Growth Hormone Use

- Elevated blood glucose
- Enlargement of liver and spleen
- Altered facial features

## IGF (SOMATOMEDIN)

Growth hormone does little on its own. Most of its actions come from a molecule called IGF-1 (insulin-dependent growth factor-1), or somatomedin. Growth hormone stimulates the liver to produce this protein, which goes to the tissues to cause most of the biological effects of growth hormone. Like growth hormone, it is a protein. Some nutritional supplement companies are selling this compound as an alternative anabolic agent. Unlike growth hormone that users inject directly into the bloodstream, IGFs are usually sold as pills. It's likely that somatomedin pills don't work because the stomach probably breaks down this protein, like others.

## GHB AND OTHER GROWTH-HORMONE RELEASING AGENTS

GHB, or gamma hydroxbutyrate, is a drug with a double life. It is used in "rave" circles as a sedative drug that causes a high like alcohol. It also has a reputation among body builders as a drug that can naturally enhance growth-hormone release from the pituitary gland and/or burn fat. GHB indeed can release a tiny amount of growth hormone from the pituitary gland. However, the burst of growth hormone lasts only minutes, and the size of the increase is very small compared to growth hormone injections. It's pretty unlikely that these drugs increase growth hormone enough to increase muscle deposition.

GHB overdoses can be lethal. GHB occurs naturally in the body, and it might actually be involved in triggering hibernation and other natural states of sedation. However, we have very little idea how this drug works or what it really does to normal brain function. GHB is used in Europe to treat narcolepsy (a sleep disorder) and as an anesthetic. At recreational doses GHB acts like alcohol, and at higher doses it can cause seizures, suppression of breathing, and coma. So many overdoses have been reported that authorities are beginning to regulate GHB as a drug of abuse.

Arginine and lysine are amino acids that are marketed as supplements promoting growth-hormone release. This claim is based on research showing that intravenous injection of a very large dose causes a spurt of growth-hormone secretion. No credible research has shown that pills accomplish this, and the amounts that people take as supplements may be too small to produce even the blip of growth-hormone release seen in the laboratory studies. So these supplements are not much more than a scam.

Some other drugs including propranolol, clonidine, and alpha-methyldopa have been used in the past to test growth hormone release in patients. All of these drugs have prominent effects on the nervous system, and taking them for growth hormone release carries too many other effects with it. Propranolol blocks the messages that the sympathetic nervous system normally sends to the heart, and it can make asthma worse. Clonidine and alpha-methyldopa lower blood pressure and cause drowsiness.

*GROWTH HORMONE THE NATURAL WAY: GET A GOOD NIGHT'S SLEEP*

Forget arginine or GHB or IGF-1. There is a very simple way to cause natural release of growth hormone: get a good night's sleep. Most growth hormone is released at night, in pulses that are separated by a couple of hours. The size of these pulses can be almost as big as the pulse caused by intravenous arginine. The biggest pulse comes at the beginning of a stage of sleep called *slow-wave sleep,* a very deep sleep that occurs about an hour to an hour and a half after you fall asleep. So spare your pocketbook, and just get a good eight hours of sleep.

## Clenbuterol

Clenbuterol is a stimulant that works on the beta receptor system of the sympathetic nervous system. It is not an anabolic steroid. Clenbuterol can increase protein content in the muscles of certain food animals, including sheep and cows (chickens, for some reason, don't respond that way). Clenbuterol can also decrease body fat in these same animals. In animal production circles, "repartioning agents" like this are incredibly popular because they change body composition to a higher percentage of protein and lower fat that increases the economic value of the animals. Yet clenbuterol is now illegal in food animals after a few highly publicized incidents in which people who ate beef or veal from clenbuterol-fed animals experienced increased heart rates, muscle tremors, dizziness, and nausea—all from drug that had accumulated in the meat. Clenbuterol has also become the scandal of livestock shows due to its use to "bulk up" champion bulls.

Athletes were quick to discover the reports of protein-increasing and fat-decreasing effects, and clenbuterol has become popular for "fat stripping" before competitions. This drug is not approved for medical use in the United States, and use by European athletes has so far exceeded use by American athletes—though American use is increasing. Unfortunately, clenbuterol may just be good for looks. It definitely makes muscles bigger, but it doesn't make them stronger or increase endurance. In fact, some animal studies show that while it makes muscles bigger, it makes endurance worse.

Why does this stimulant but not others make muscles bigger? The difference may simply be in how long it lasts, plus the balance of its actions on different organ systems. Clenbuterol can be used to treat asthma because it dilates bronchioles. It also improves blood flow to muscle, slightly stimulates the heart, causes breakdown of fat, and may slightly increase the rate of metabolism. If it were inhaled, not enough would be delivered to the muscles to do much. But when people ingest it, it lasts a long time. Besides the time-course issue, we really don't know why it increases muscle mass, and why it does so more than other stimulants. The oral route unfortunately also guarantees that clenbuterol will have more side effects than normal asthma medicine. It can increase heart rate and cause jitteriness, just like in the people who ate contaminated meat.

## Creatine Phosphate

Dietary supplementation with creatine is the current rage for everyone from weekend joggers to pro football players, who take it to improve endurance. As we discussed in Chapter 1, muscles need ATP to contract, but muscle stores of ATP itself last only a second. Creatine phosphate provides the next line of defense by providing phosphate for ATP resupply. The creatine phosphate supplies of normal muscles can maintain activity for several seconds more than ATP stores alone. Creatine should speed recovery after a single, very brief burst of energy use like at the start of a sprint, and speed recovery between sprinting episodes, and so improve performance on repeat brief sprints. It might also help in performance of single brief exercise, although the key word here is brief (five to ten seconds).

Here is a short summary of the studies to date of creatine supplementation on muscle function:

1. Creatine supplementation definitely increases the amount
   of creatine and phosphocreatine in the muscle. The typical
   "loading" strategy of 10 to 20 grams/day for five days followed by maintenance of 2 to 3 grams/day for a month
   causes an increase in muscle creatine content from 5 to 15
   percent. It takes about a month for creatine levels to fall all
   the way back to normal after supplements are stopped.

2. Creatine increases body weight, but it may not increase
   muscle mass. Much of the weight gain may well be water
   held in the muscle with the creatine, not muscle mass.

3. Performance on closely spaced repeat sprintlike activities
   are those most reliably improved. Although there are many
   positive and negative findings for swimming sprints, rowing
   sprints, brief lifting "sprints," and running sprints, there are
   at least a few credible studies that report improvements.
   There are studies of every kind of person: highly trained
   athletes, formerly sedentary young people, elderly people
   on weight training, etc. Highly-trained athletes seem to be
   most likely to show benefits.

4. When performance improvements occur, they are slight—
   in the range of 1 to 5 percent. This explains why some studies brag more about their results than others. A 1 percent
   improvement in a swimming time in a 100-yard sprint (or
   0.5 to 1.5 seconds) is a huge improvement, but under other
   circumstances it doesn't mean much.

5. Creatine phosphate does not significantly improve endurance
   during aerobic exercise. Exercise that is sustained for more
   than a minute or so relies on aerobic metabolism, not on
   creatine phosphate. Athletes who cycle or run long dis-
   tances should just forget it.

There are still lots of unknowns about creatine supplementation. The relative failure of creatine supplements to improve endurance-like performance is a little surprising. One philosophy of creatine supplementation is that it permits faster recovery during repetitions of bursts of activities. This should permit more repetitions in each set and more total repetitions in a workout—for example, repeat lifting bouts. However, we haven't seen this result consistently. This might be a limitation in the design of the scientific studies or a limitation built in to the way people work out. Athletes might simply become fatigued or stop before they experience the benefit.

We don't know if creatine use during training prevents normal helpful adaptations that training causes in the muscle. The purpose of training is to induce the body to make adaptations that make exercise easier the next time. Training normally increases the enzymes that make creatine phosphate: training alone can increase creatine stores as much as 30 percent, a change comparable to that claimed by dietary supplements. Though still unproven, it is likely that the muscle's inducement to make its own changes is removed by dietary supplementation. This would make the athlete's body dependent on supplements instead of responsive to training.

A note on drug combinations: Most studies do not investigate combinations. At least one study that compared creatine with creatine plus caffeine noted that all the benefits provided by creatine were negated by caffeine—bad news for dietary supplements that provide both.

# Insulin and Oral Hypoglycemic Drugs

Insulin is the main hormone in the body that regulates blood sugar (glucose). After a meal, the pancreas releases insulin, which allows cells to take up the glucose provided by the meal to use it for energy. Diabetes is the disease that results from the lack of insulin or insensitivity to its actions. Diabetic people can't take glucose up into cells to use it for energy, so blood glucose levels rise, but the body thinks it doesn't have enough, so it keeps trying to produce more. Fat and protein stores in the body are used up instead to produce glucose in the liver. Insulin also has some other effects, including stimulating the uptake of amino acids, the precursors of proteins, into muscle. This is the action that athletes try to enhance by injecting insulin in conjunction with workouts.

Athletes use insulin to get amino acid uptake into muscle with the idea that providing some more amino acids will promote muscle growth. This is probably ineffective and definitely very dangerous. It is easy to overdose on insulin and drive blood glucose to dangerously low levels. Most athletes who use insulin have experienced the racing heartbeat, clammy skin, and nausea associated with low blood glucose. Since the brain needs glucose for energy, if blood glucose falls too low, coma and even death can result.

There is another side effect of taking insulin that most athletes would want to avoid, anyway. Since insulin slows the breakdown of fat, taking extra insulin can lead to more fat deposition, especially at the site of insulin injection. Many diabetics experience this problem unless they are careful to inject themselves in a different spot each time they take insulin for their diabetes.

## Chromium Piccolinate

Chromium is an element that is marketed as piccolinate salt in many weight-loss and/or muscle-building products. This marketing is based on some intriguing but preliminary research showing that chromium improves insulin sensitivity in diabetics. The possibility of improving insulin effects in these patients who don't respond well to the drug on its own offers some real hope for treatment.

The jury is still out about how much chromium helps insulin action, and in what sorts of people. Research is really just beginning. Some studies have shown promising effects of chromium in diabetic patients, but others have failed to show any benefit to chromium supplements. The few studies using athletes have not shown any effects of chromium on measures of lean body mass or athletic performance.

Chromium is available in the diet, especially in mushrooms, prunes, nuts, whole-grain bread and cereal, and Brewer's yeast. Some nutritionists argue that the average American diet provides only about half of the 50 to 200 micrograms needed daily. Most multivitamins provide chromium in this range.

## Amino Acid Supplements

Body-building magazines are packed with ads for numerous products containing protein in various forms, from complete protein to isolated amino acids. Most of these magazines claim that athletes must take nutritional supplements to get maximal muscle

development during training. Nutritionists almost always pooh-
pooh this idea, claiming that the average American diet is so full
of protein that nobody eating this standard diet is protein deficient, even someone engaging in vigorous physical training.
While this is probably true, the story is a little more complicated
than that. It *is* possible that certain athletes, especially those on
extreme low-carbohydrate–low-fat diets, might need more protein than others because they need protein both to build protein
and for energy.

Amino acids are the building blocks of proteins. When we eat
proteins, the acid and enzymes in our stomach and intestines
break them down into their constituent amino acids, which are
absorbed and used throughout the body in the production of new
proteins, including contractile proteins in the muscle. There are
twenty-two amino acids, and we need all twenty-two to make protein, so taking supplements of isolated amino acids usually doesn't
do any good for building proteins. Amino acids can also be converted to glucose in the liver or muscle, or enter the pathway for
energy metabolism for fats at various stages. The liver uses amino
acids as a source of energy when glycogen is gone. Tryptophan,
tyrosine, glutamic acid, aspartic acid, and proline are the building
blocks for certain neurotransmitters in the brain, as well, and they
are often marketed as mood boosters for that reason.


## SOURCES OF AMINO ACIDS

The best sources of protein have all the essential amino acids in
an ideal ratio and are highly digestible, but not all foods provide
all the essential amino acids. Animal proteins in general are better
than others, but even these vary. Eggs come closest to being the

## Thyroid Hormone Preparations Obtained from Medical Sources

1. **Synthroid**
125 mcg, Knoll
Pharmaceutical
Company.

---

## Anabolic Steroids

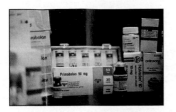

2. Abusers may use a variety of anabolic steroids during a cycle.

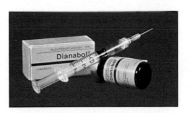

6. **Dianabol**. Controlled ingredient: methandrostenoleone 25 mg/ml.

3. Counterfeiters duplicate packaging for black market sales.

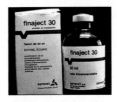

7. **Finajet**. Controlled ingredient: trenbolone acetate.

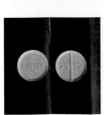

4. **Andadrol**. Controlled ingredient: oxymetholone 50 mg.

8. **Parabolin**. Controlled ingredient: trenbolone 50 mg.

5. **Android**-25. Controlled ingredient: methytestosterone 25 mg.

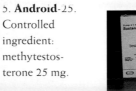

9. **Sustanon**. Controlled ingredient: testosterone esters 250 mg.

## Anabolic Steroids, continued

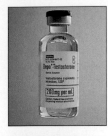

10. **Depo-Testosterone**. Controlled ingredient: testosterone cypionate 100 mg/ml.

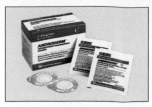

13. **Androderm** (testosterone transdermal system), SmithKline Beecham Pharmaceuticals.

11. **Testosterone**. Controlled ingredient: testosterone 200 mg/ml.

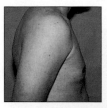

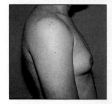

14. **"Bitch tits"** (gynecomastia) is a condition of abnormal breast development, which can be caused by a number of factors including anabolic steroid or marijuana use. The only known treatment is surgical removal of the excess tissue.

12. **Winstrol**. Controlled ingredient: stanozolol 2 mg/ml.

---

**Gonadotropin Releasing Hormone: Used at the end of an anabolic steroid cycle to stimulate the person's own testosterone production**

15. **Lupron Depot** 4 Month 30 mg, Tap Pharmaceuticals Inc.

---

**Growth Hormone Preparations Obtained from Medical Sources**

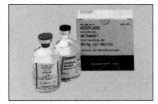

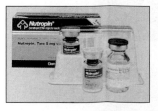

17. **Nutropin** 5 mg, approx. 30 IU, packaged with 10 mL multi-dose vial of bacteriostatic water (benzyl alcohol preserved), Genentech, Inc.

16. **Activase** 50 mg, 29 million IU, packaged with diluent, Genentech, Inc.

## Stimulants: Used as drugs of abuse, anorectic drugs, ADHD or performance-enhancing drugs

18. **Dexedrine.** Controlled ingredient: dextroamphetamine sulfate 10 mg.

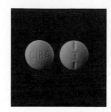

19. **Ritalin.** Controlled ingredient: methylphenidate hydrochloride 10 mg.

## Prescription Bronchodilators

20. **Ventolin Nebules** inhalation solution 0.083%, Glaxo Wellcome Inc.

22. **Theo-Dur** 300 mg, Key Pharmaceuticals.

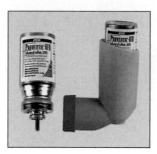

21. **Proventil HFA**, Key Pharmaceuticals.

## Erythropoietin (EPO): Used by athletes to increase red blood cell numbers

23. **Epogen**, Amgen Inc.

24. **Procrit**, Ortho Biotech Inc.

## Marijuana

25. Marijuana abusers prefer the *colas*, or buds of the plant, because of its higher THC content. Leaves are now discarded or used as filler. The effects of THC in the body can be detected weeks after smoking.

## Sedative Drugs

## Narcotic Pain Killers

26. **Valium**. Controlled ingredient: diazepam 5 mg.

30. **Percodan**. Controlled ingredients: oxycodone hydrochloride 4.5 mg, oxycodone terephthalate 0.38 mg. Other ingredient: aspirin 325 mg.

27. **Xanax**. Controlled ingredient: alprazolam 0.5 mg.

28. **Halcion**. Controlled ingredient: triazolam 0.25 mg

31. **Tylenol** with Codeine No. 3. Controlled ingredient: codeine phosphate 30 mg. Other ingredient: acetaminophen 300 mg.

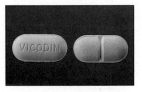

29. **Rohyphnol** ("roofies"), the famous "date-rape" drug, can cause unconsciousness and amnesia, especially in combination with alcohol. Contains the controlled ingredient flunitrazepam hydrochloride.

32. **Vicodin**. Controlled ingredient: hydrocodone bitartrate 5 mg. Other ingredient: acetaminophen 500 mg.

**N.B.: Prescription drugs with valid medical uses are sometimes diverted to illegal use by athletes. They normally can be obtained only by a prescription from a physician.**

perfect protein source, followed closely by milk. Beef and peanuts are equivalent, and other plant products provide only about one-third to one-half the protein value of eggs.

Some major plant proteins lack certain essential amino acids. Grains like corn and wheat are relatively deficient in lysine and isoleucine, while legumes are poor in tryptophan. The common combination of corn and beans in some diets provides complementary amino acids. Together they form a complete protein source. The peasant cuisines of many cultures reflects this: rice and beans or corn and beans in Mexico and South America, for example, or pasta and lentils or beans in southern Italy. Those of you who watched the movie *Jurassic Park* will remember that essential amino acids were a vital plot device. The dinosaurs were genetically engineered to require a source of lysine, which the animal caretakers were supposed to provide. Clever animals that they were, they figured it out and ate plants rich in lysine, thereby escaping control of their human caretakers and providing the basis for a sequel.

## HOW MUCH PROTEIN?

Simply eating protein doesn't stimulate muscle formation. Muscle formation is stimulated by exercise, and the amount of muscle produced depends on genetics and hormones. Eating protein, or drinking amino-acid drinks, will not make you muscular, and if you ingest much more protein than you need, the body will convert some of it to fat. Athletes who exercise intensely break down some muscle protein and need somewhat more protein than inactive people. In addition, athletes who are trying to deposit muscle need a little more protein to allow new muscle formation. The exact amount required depends on how much the athlete exercises, plus how much protein is normally eaten. Some exercise physiologists guess that at most, athletes in training need double the requirements of more sedentary folk.

Even heavily training athletes can easily consume enough protein in the average American diet. Men need between 50 and 60 grams of protein daily, depending on their age, and women need between 40 and 50 grams. If we add up the protein content of an average American diet using charts available from nutrition textbooks (our source is *Nutrition Facts Manual, A Quick Reference*, A. S. Bloch, M. E. Shils, Williams and Wilkins, Baltimore, 1996), it is suprisingly easy to achieve this total.

A typical day of meals for a female athlete who is trying to maximize protein intake and minimize fat might look like this:

| | |
|---|---|
| Breakfast: skim milk, 2 eggs, 1 piece of toast | 16.8 grams of protein |
| Lunch: skim milk, chicken breast sandwich, tomato | 16.3 grams of protein |
| Dinner: skim milk, halibut, potatoes, beans | 19.2 grams of protein |
| **Total** | **52.3 grams of protein** |

She has achieved her protein goal without trying very hard. These numbers are probably underestimates: they assume very small portions, such as only an ounce of meat, and 8 ounces of milk. But Americans rarely serve as little as 1 ounce of meat, and most glasses accommodate more than 8 ounces of liquid. More typical servings would result in protein intake of almost 100 grams. This supports nutritionists' claims that no one on a normal American diet needs protein supplements.

Then there is cost to consider. On a recent research trip to a local grocery store and mall, we found that the average cost of 10 grams of protein in the form of eggs is about 14¢. Protein supplements at mall nutritional supplement stores cost from 21¢ to more than $1. The $1 item was an egg-protein product, and so it was the most directly comparable. This is a price differential of sevenfold. In addition to cost, the nutritional value of these items is obviously different. The egg-protein powder had no fat (a good thing) but no other nutrients, either.

Many supplement manufacturers tout the value of eating purified amino acid mixtures instead of protein to avoid the metabolic cost and inefficiency of digestion. This is bunk. The digestive system is designed to break proteins down into their component amino acids fast enough to make amino acids available for protein synthesis.

Heavily training athletes probably do have higher protein requirements than sedentary people. However, these needs are not ten times higher but at most maybe double. It's easy to get enough protein in a balanced diet. But if athletes don't want to pay attention to their diet, or are trying to minimize calorie intake severely, then supplements could be helpful.

## DIETING BEFORE WEIGHT-LIFTING COMPETITIONS: AMINO ACIDS AND ENERGY

Many body builders eat extremely low-calorie diets just before a major competition in order to get optimal definition of muscles. When carbohydrates aren't available in the diet, the body burns muscle protein for energy, tearing down muscles, which is exactly what the athletes don't want. In these situations, they need to be particularly attentive to their protein intake to avoid breaking down muscle protein for energy.

## Specific Amino Acids

More and more reports claim benefits of specific amino acids on muscle deposition or on muscle recovery after exercise. Leucine, isoleucine, and valine are touted as critical for recovery, and arginine and ornithine are marketed for their ability to release growth hormone. What is the basis for these claims?

We have already discussed the reason that amino acids are probably not very useful for releasing growth hormone (see p. 91). In terms of "muscle recovery," protein synthesis can't take place without all the amino acids, so a single amino acid won't help there. The amino acid derivative glutamine has become a part of many nutritional supplements. Glutamine is the most abundant amino acid in the blood. Solid research in humans shows that it serves as primary source of glucose production in the kidneys. A couple of animal studies report that it can promote muscle glycogen deposition in animals and it perhaps can promote protein synthesis. However, benefits in muscle deposition or indices of fitness have never been shown in humans.

Some product claims are based on the use of amino acids for energy as well as muscle building. For example, "branched chain" amino acids like isoleucine and leucine are the first to be used for energy after an intense workout. Similarly, a breakdown product of leucine, β-hydroxy β-methylbutyrate is supposed to improve muscle size by inhibiting protein breakdown during training. Although one human study in nonathletes who were beginning a training regimen reported this result, others have failed to replicate this finding.

If an athlete is eating a normal diet, there is no strong evidence right now that taking these bizarre products provides a benefit in terms of muscle deposition or athletic performance. A glass of fruit juice or perhaps a yogurt/fruit smoothie that provided a little glucose and protein would probably be just as good or better for energy, and mixed protein like that found in dairy products or animal proteins will provide for both muscle repair and energy. In fact, some solid research shows that a carbohydrate meal after training improves some biochemical markers of muscle damage and recovery. However, there are no studies showing effects of such nutritional strategies on performance measures or muscle size.

## The Bottom Line

1. Steroids can increase muscle mass but only at doses that have potentially dangerous effects on the heart, brain, and reproductive tract.
2. Growth hormone and drugs that supposedly release growth hormone provide at best limited and more likely no benefit for performance.
3. Creatine can increase performance during extremely brief bursts of exercise, when energy production depends on creatine stores.
4. Chromium and most other micronutrients are of no proven benefit to athletic performance.
5. The best diet for overall athletic performance is one with adequate protein for muscle repair and building, plus adequate carbohydrate for energy production. Specific supplements are not necessary.

# Chapter 6

# GETTING
# PUMPED

## CONTENTS

The Sympathetic Nervous System and Athletic
    Performance
The Chemical Kick of the SNS: Activation of the
    "Adrenaline" System
Stimulants as an Aid to Training: The Risk/Reward
    Equation
How Stimulants Work
Cocaine
Amphetamine
Ephedrine (Ma Huang, "Herbal Ecstasy")
ADHD, Ritalin, and Sports
Bronchodilators
Decongestants
Caffeine
    *Does It Work? Is It Safe?*

*continued on next page*

Does Caffeine Improve Athletic Performance?
WHAT ARE THE DANGERS OF CAFFEINE?
WHAT ABOUT THE CONSEQUENCES OF LONG-TERM USE?
Tolerance to Stimulants
Blood Doping and EPO
The Bottom Line

Q U I Z
## Match the names to the actions

| | |
|---|---|
| *Amphetamine* | The most widely used psychoactive drug in |
| *Ephedrine* | the United States |
| *Pseudoephedrine* | A nasal decongestant |
| *Albuterol* | A highly addictive drug of abuse |
| *Caffeine* | An ancient Chinese herbal drug |
| | An asthma drug |

Now, which of these stimulant drugs are used by athletes?

This list of drugs includes a highly addictive drug of abuse (amphetamine), an "herbal" drug used by thousands (ephedrine), a nasal decongestant that hockey players use to "get up" for a game (pseudoephedrine), a safe and effective asthma drug (albuterol), and the most widely used psychoactive drug in the United States (caffeine). These drugs are all stimulants of one form or another, and athletes use all of them to increase attention and concentration, prolong exercise times, and improve aerobic capacity.

People have used stimulants to improve physical performance for as long as they have understood what these drugs did. Native populations in South America have chewed coca leaves (which contain cocaine) to provide energy and improve endurance for thousands of years, and the practice continues today. Amphetamine was developed by Eli Lilly corporation in the 1920s as a substitute for ephedrine in the treatment of asthma, and physicians started using it for nasal decongestion, to increase alertness, and as an appetite suppressant. Amphetamine use by endurance athletes began almost as soon as marketing of the drug began in the 1930s, and even pilots in World War II used it to improve vigilance. Caffeine, in coffee or tea, is used by much of the world's population every day to increase alertness. These drugs all have something in common: they stimulate the sympathetic nervous system (SNS).

## *The Sympathetic Nervous System and Athletic Performance*

The SNS prepares the body for "flight or fight." Part of the SNS in the brain helps a person pay attention to the environment (looking for threats); the other part goes to the organs to prepare the body to flee if the threat is too great. The SNS dilates the pupils to let more light in, widens the bronchioles to provide more oxygen, increases heart rate, and diverts blood to the muscles to prepare for running. It also breaks down glucose and fat to provide energy for these muscles. It does this both directly and by changing the levels of the hormones insulin and glucagon.

These actions of the SNS are just what the body needs during exercise. They improve the intake of sensory information by the brain, increase the delivery of oxygen to muscles, and increase the delivery of nutrients to muscles. The SNS does not increase strength, but by making more nutrients available to muscles, it increases the capacity for work and probably the duration of exercise.

## The Chemical Kick of the SNS: Activation of the "Adrenaline" System

The neurons of the SNS release a chemical neurotransmitter called *norepinephrine* (or noradrenaline), which creates all the effects described above. Norepinephrine neurons in the brain regulate alertness and mood as well as body temperature and appetite. They also make contact with organs outside the nervous system to trigger the effects on cardiovascular function, glucose availability, etc. One special part of the SNS, the inner part of the adrenal gland, called the *adrenal medulla*, releases a very similar neurotransmitter called *epinephrine* (or adrenaline). Epinephrine enters the bloodstream during stress or during intense exercise. It does the same thing that norepinephrine does. Norepinephrine and epinephrine act together to produce the changes that prepare the body for exercise. The adrenal gland produces epinephrine during stress to provide a little extra boost. All the drugs used as stimulants except caffeine mimic the actions of the SNS.

You have probably heard that adrenaline (epinephrine) is what makes people feel nervous before an event. This isn't exactly correct. Epinephrine makes your heart beat faster, and people associate the heart pounding with feeling anxious. But the fact is, while stress triggers both the release of epinephrine and feelings of alertness or anxiety, it triggers them at the same time; one doesn't cause the other. Epinephrine doesn't enter the brain, where norepinephrine neurons create feelings like alertness or anxiety.

The following is a list of bodily functions that are relevant to physical performance and are strongly influenced by norepinephrine and epinephrine through the SNS:

*Eye*        Dilation of pupil: improved vision
*Bronchiole*  Dilation of muscle: increased oxygen uptake
*Heart*      Increase in rate and force of contraction

*Blood vessels*
*Skin*        Contraction: decrease blood flow to skin
*Organs*      Contraction: decrease blood flow
*Muscle*      Relaxation: increase blood blow

*Liver*       Release of glucose from glycogen, synthesize glucose from free fatty acids
*Fat*         Breakdown of fats (lipolysis)
*Pancreas*    Release of glucagon, inhibition of insulin: hormone effects that increase blood glucose

Norepinephrine and epinephrine can do all of these different jobs in the body because they interact with many slightly different receptors. By contrast, the numerous drugs related to norepinephrine tend to be more specialized. Some work only in the lungs to dilate the bronchioles, while others only constrict blood vessels.

There are two important groups of receptors related to norepinephrine and epinephrine. Alpha receptors constrict blood vessels and increase heart rate, while beta receptors increase the force of contraction of the heart, dilate bronchioles, release stores of glucose and fatty acids, and dilate blood vessels. Drugs that work on alpha receptors are good for stuffy noses, and drugs that work on beta receptors are good for asthma.

## Stimulants as an Aid to Training: The Risk/Reward Equation

Exercise activates the SNS naturally. The greater the demand created by exercise, the greater the activation of the SNS. Levels of norepinephrine in the circulation can increase five- or tenfold during maximal exercise. This is a very important consideration in evaluating the actions of stimulants. For an athlete training under less than maximal conditions, amplification of SNS activity might cause some benefit. However, for athletes performing under maximally stressful conditions, most of these drugs probably don't add that much. Those that have a real impact, like amphetamine, can cause such dangerous excesses of norepinephrine that heart attacks or stroke can result. Even during training, there is a downside to stimulant use. One of the desired outcomes of training is to stress muscles that are exercising so that their need for oxygen and nutrients activates the SNS. If athletes use drugs instead of exercise to activate the SNS, then the appropriate adaptations may not happen during training.

## How Stimulants Work

The drugs we listed in our quiz at the beginning of the chapter vary from doing everything that the SNS does (amphetamine) to having a very specific action like constriction of blood vessels. These differences are caused by their chemical structures which determine whether the drug can enter the brain and which receptors it will activate. These actions determine the effects that a drug will have on the body.

Cocaine, amphetamine, caffeine, and ephedrine can enter the brain and produce effects on behavior. Their chemical structures allow these drugs to pass through cells easily and so they can pass through the "blood brain barrier" that surrounds the brain and prevents the entrance of many chemicals. Other stimulants that are often used by athletes can't enter the brain or do so poorly. Therefore, they are not effective at improving vigilance, nor do they carry the risk of addiction. Athletes sometimes compensate by taking huge doses of these drugs in the hopes of getting a little into the brain—a risky practice since it leads to excessive effects in other parts of the body.

Cocaine, amphetamine, and ephedrine all increase the amount of norepinephrine that's available to stimulate the receptors. By getting inside the norepinephrine neurons and releasing the norepinephrine, or by preventing its recapture by the neuron, they stimulate the SNS all over the entire body, producing the whole gamut of "flight or fight" responses. They increase heart rate and blood pressure, they increase blood flow to the muscle, decrease blood flow to the internal organs and skin, and increase blood glucose and free fatty acids.

The following table lists many of the stimulants banned by the U.S. Olympic Committee (USOC) and the International Olympic Committee (IOC). They are listed in groupings according to their usual clinical use. The table indicates whether they enter the brain, whether they have the indirect action of increasing norepinephrine, and whether they increase alpha and/or beta effects. All drugs that increase norepinephrine have both alpha and beta effects because norepinephrine does both things. Drugs that are not marketed in the United States but only in Europe, are not listed here.

| Drug | Enter Brain | Increase NE | Alpha Effects | Beta Effects |
| --- | --- | --- | --- | --- |
| **Nonprescription Drugs** | | | | |
| Cocaine | X | +++ | X | X |
| Ephedrine or | | | | |
| Ma Huang | X | +++ | X | X |
| | | | | |
| **Drugs Used to Treat ADHD** | | | | |
| Amphetamine | X | +++ | X | X |
| Methylphenidate | X | ++ | X | X |
| Pemoline | X | | | |
| | | | | |
| **Drugs Used to Treat Obesity** | | | | |
| Methamphetamine | X | +++ | X | X |
| Phentermine | X | ++ | X | X |
| | | | | |
| **Drugs Used to Treat Asthma** | | | | |
| Isoetharine | | | | X |
| Isoproterenol | | | | X |
| Metaproterenol | | | | X |
| | | | | |
| **Nasal Decongestants** | | | | |
| Desoxyephedrine | | | X | |
| Phenylpro- | | | | |
| panolamine | +/- | | X | |
| Propylhexedrine | | | X | |
| Pseudoephedrine | | | X | |

The effectiveness of these drugs also reflects their risks. All the drugs that increase norepinephrine carry the risk of overstimulation of the cardiovascular system, raising blood pressure and heart rate and predisposing the athlete to disturbance of heart rhythm or other cardiovascular injury.

## Cocaine

Cocaine may well be the original performance-enhancing stimulant. Since at least the sixth century, South American native populations have chewed the leaves of the coca plant, which contain the active ingredient cocaine, in order to improve endurance. When the Spaniards conquered the Incas in the sixteenth century, they paid the natives in coca leaves for working in the silver mines. This was an ideal bargain, from the point of view of the conquerors, because the cocaine allowed the workers to work longer in the mines. When cocaine was brought to Europe, it was first used as a general "tonic" to increase energy. Sigmund Freud created the first known cocaine addict when he used it to wean his friend Dr. Ernst von Fleischl-Marxow from a morphine addiction. He was also the first investigator to study the effects of cocaine on athletic performance (he conducted a series of experiments upon himself to determine whether cocaine increased muscular strength). Cocaine use in sports dates to the late 1800s, when it was used (in combination with opiate drugs) by bicyclists in endurance races. Cocaine now appears most frequently in the sports pages as a drug of recreational abuse by high-profile athletes.

Chewing coca leaves releases cocaine slowly into the circulation. This is an ideal way to provide consistent levels of cocaine in the blood for a long time, but it's a poor way to produce the "rush" and rapid high that is so appealing to recreational users. In contrast, purified cocaine can be delivered quickly in high quantities by hypodermic needle, snorting, or smoking as crack. In these forms, cocaine enters the body very quickly and leaves quickly, leading to the high followed by a crash that every crack smoker recognizes. Purification of cocaine ruined its use for enhanced physical performance and endurance. Every country that marketed cocaine tonics experienced a rash of abuse cases and overdoses, until eventually the cocaine in tonic—including Coca Cola!—was banned almost everywhere.

Cocaine increases all the actions of the SNS. It increases heart rate, constricts blood vessels, increases the supply of glucose and lipid in the circulation, and dilates the bronchioles. Cocaine is still used in nasal surgery to produce constriction of blood vessels in the nose to prevent bleeding during surgery. It also enters the brain very well and causes the arousal, diminished appetite, and altered hormone function that norepinephrine triggers in the brain.

Cocaine does this by preventing the removal of norepinephrine from the gap between neurons where it acts. Keeping the neurotransmitter active for a longer period increases the effects of every neuron in the SNS. However, the rapid entry and removal of cocaine in its modern, purified forms from the system means that these effects don't last very long. This is one reason that cocaine is not useful for performance enhancement.

The other reason that purified cocaine isn't very useful for athletic performance is that it has additional effects that aren't helpful to athletes. Addictiveness is the biggest problem. Many people who start using cocaine develop a compulsive, out-of-control habit of use that can take over their lives. This effect is completely separate from its effects on the SNS. Cocaine is addictive because it acts on dopamine neurons in the brain along with norepinephrine neurons. Dopamine is a neurotransmitter very similar to norepinephrine, but it exists in very different places in the brain and acts on the reward system—the part of the brain that allows a person to feel pleasure. It is no surprise that addicts say that injecting or smoking cocaine is like having sex because having sex also makes dopamine levels in this part of the brain go up.

All drugs that are addictive (cocaine, amphetamine, nicotine, alcohol, and heroin) stimulate dopamine neurons, one way or another. Cocaine does it directly, by doing the same for dopamine that it does for norepinephrine: it keeps dopamine around longer, once it is released, by blocking the normal processes that return dopamine to the neurons. Cocaine also increases levels of serotonin. Serotonin is that neurotransmitter that is enhanced by the popular antidepressants called *selective serotonin reuptake inhibitors* (SSRIs) like Prozac and Zoloft. Cocaine causes appetite suppression and changes in hormone levels partly due to serotonin effects.

The other big problem with cocaine use by athletes is that cocaine can act like a local anesthetic. This property helps when it is used in nasal surgery because patients not only bleed less, they feel less pain. However, local anesthetic effects are responsible for some of the most dangerous toxicities of cocaine overdose. In the heart they can lead to a fatal disturbance of the heartbeat, and in the brain they are probably what leads to the seizures associated with overdoses.

## Amphetamine

Amphetamine was developed by chemists at the Eli Lilly drug company in the 1930s in an attempt to develop an ephedrine-like drug that worked better but had less dangerous side effects.

Amphetamine certainly works better than ephedrine in every way, but it is also more dangerous. Amphetamine has been used to enhance performance almost since its introduction into medicine. It has been used by armies to increase alertness and vigilance in the field and by groups as diverse as truck drivers and cyclists to improve attention and endurance.

Amphetamine acts very much like cocaine, but it has even more dramatic effects. It enters the brain quickly, where it increases alertness, and people who take amphetamine are talkative, energetic, and move around a lot. It was used as an appetite suppressant before doctors realized how additive it is. As highly addictive as cocaine, amphetamine produces a rush of pleasure if taken in an injectable or smoked form. When people take amphetamine in very high quantities for prolonged times, a paranoid psychotic state emerges that is virtually indistinguishable from schizophrenia. This state clears up when amphetamine use stops, but it can persist if a person continues to use it. In the body, amphetamine increases heart rate and blood pressure, dilates the bronchioles, increases glucose and fatty acids in the bloodstream, and generally acts like an overall stimulant of the SNS.

Like cocaine, amphetamine causes these effects by increasing the amount of norepinephrine and dopamine available to bind to receptors. However, it acts a little differently. Amphetamine goes directly into the neurons, then actively dumps the neurotransmitters out of the neuron. The end result is much bigger changes in these neurotransmitters than cocaine causes, and greater behavioral and physiologic effects. For example, the effects of amphetamine can lead to a dangerous increase in body temperature that cocaine rarely causes, *especially during exercise.*

Studies in the 1940s and 50s, soon after the first marketing of amphetamine, provide some insight into what amphetamine does for athletic performance. The pronounced increase in alertness caused by the effects of amphetamine in the brain can permit sustained attention to boring, repetitive tasks. This allows the athlete to focus on the activity, either during training or during an event. But the increased energy and sense of euphoria can "mask" natural warnings of fatigue and pain that would stop an injured or tiring athlete when the body's resources are failing.

Amphetamine and methamphetamine are sold as medicines and so are found in pill form. They are also synthesized in bootleg laboratories, usually as loose crystals, or rocks. Production of methamphetamine in bootleg labs has skyrocketed recently. The powder or crystal form is either snorted or dissolved and injected intravenously. The rocks are smoked, much like crack cocaine. In any form, the effects of amphetamine last much longer than those of cocaine: one dose can have an impact for four to six hours.

Amphetamine use presents many risks to the athlete. When it is used during training or an event, the significant overstimulation of the cardiovascular system may lead to a fatal disturbance of heart rhythm. Stroke is also a risk. In addition, amphetamine, unlike other stimulants, can increase body temperature to dangerous levels during intense exercise.

Although use during training carries the risk of immediate death, the long-term risks are almost as bad. Amphetamine and methamphetamine are highly addictive—as much so as cocaine. Long-term, high-dose use can cause dramatic loss of body weight due to inhibited appetite; damage to the heart can develop because of excessive stimulation by norepinephrine; and, as mentioned above, a state resembling paranoid schizophrenia involving anxiety, restlessness, and delusions of persecution can emerge. Amphetamine stimulates bizarre grooming patterns in which people pick at their skin until it bleeds. Most of these effects reverse when amphetamine use stops, but the heart damage can be irreversible. Amphetamine abusers can develop pathologically enlarged hearts (cardiomyopathy). In addition, some new evidence has shown that dopamine neurons can be permanently damaged by long-term high-dose use of amphetamine.


## Ephedrine (Ma Huang, "Herbal Ecstasy")

Ephedrine in the form of the herbal preparation Ma Huang has been used to treat asthma in Asia for thousands of years and is still used today. Ephedrine causes a dilation of the bronchioles of the lungs that improves the flow of air for asthmatic patients. Recently, ephedrine has become popular as an "herbal" recreational drug ("herbal Ecstasy"), and it's one of the most widely marketed performance-enhancing drugs. Its use by athletes is skyrocketing. In fact, it's contained in so many herbal performance-enhancing products that athletes often don't know they are taking it.

Ephedrine causes all the signs of an overall activation of the SNS: an increase in heart rate and blood pressure, dilation of the bronchioles, an increase in glucose and fatty acids in the circulation, and so on. Because it causes breakdown of fat like other drugs that stimulate the SNS, it's popular as a weight-loss aid, although clinical studies haven't shown it to be all that effective.

Ephedrine directly releases norepinephrine from neurons, much the way amphetamine does. The two big differences between ephedrine and amphetamine are that ephedrine doesn't increase dopamine, so it isn't addictive, and it doesn't enter the brain very well. It can make an athlete jittery or sleep less. But it doesn't have very big effects on the brain in comparison to amphetamine.

Some athletes swear by taking ephedrine before they work out. They believe that ephedrine builds bigger muscles. They also think that the increase in heart rate means they're getting a better workout. Both of these beliefs are simply wrong.

First, there is no evidence that ephedrine builds muscle in humans or in animals. The second misconception may be more of a problem to the athlete. Ephedrine increases heart rate by stimulating the heart directly with norepinephrine, so the athlete has the false perception of working hard. Normally, heart rate speeds up during exercise because muscles use up oxygen more quickly, and the brain increases heart rate to increase oxygen delivery to the muscles. That's why heart rate is a good index of how hard one is working out. A regular habit of ephedrine use could result in less- rather than more-challenging workouts.

Surprisingly, in some scientific studies the real benefit of ephedrine has not been in either of these areas but rather in an increase in alertness. It allows sustained attention and focus on boring tasks, and perhaps improved learning of the tasks.

Does ephedrine enhance performance during competition, even if it isn't useful during training? Competitive athletes have thought so for years. There have been numerous incidents of Olympic athletes being disqualified for use of ephedrine. In truth, ephedrine might improve performance a little by causing bronchodilation, thereby boosting oxygen delivery to tissues as well as improving glucose and fatty acid availability. These effects obviously would be of greatest benefit during sustained, aerobic exercise.

But ephedrine can be dangerous, even fatal. It is marketed widely and indiscriminately, and many athletes take toxic amounts. They experience the nervousness, anxiety, palpitations, insomnia, and tremor that are signs of overdose. When an athlete has these side effects, it's likely that his blood pressure and heart rate are increasing to levels that are potentially life-threatening. Repeated ephedrine use can lead to destruction of heart tissue and death due to heart failure.

Even young, healthy athletes have died from ephedrine use. Numerous studies in the medical literature have reported sudden cardiac death in body builders and other athletes who used ephedrine while working out. Chronic high-dose use also leads to mental effects including insomnia, nervousness, and, in extreme cases, mania. Fortunately, the FDA has recognized these effects and is starting to think about regulating the indiscriminate marketing of ephedrine in nutritional supplements.

*Signs of Excess Ephedrine Use*
- Nervousness
- Anxiety
- Insomnia
- Heart palpitations
- Tremor

## ADHD, Ritalin, and Sports

Should athletes with attention deficit hyperactivity disorder (ADHD) use their stimulant medication while competing? Amphetamine and methamphetamine are important drugs in the treatment of ADHD. Two other stimulants, pemoline and methylphenidate (Ritalin) also are used to treat ADHD in the United States. All of these drugs enter the brain and increase vigilance and attention. They all also activate the SNS. Stimulants increase alertness and attention in everybody, and this is the basis for their use in sports

that require vigilance. But what about athletes with clinically diag-
nosed ADHD who aren't "normal" without stimulants? This is a
tough question to answer. Although their brains might function normally only with the drugs present, the rest of their bodies also
receive an extra boost when taking these medications. That is the
basis for the current ban on these drugs in most sports.

## Bronchodilators

Asthma occurs when allergens, cold air, or other irritants trigger a
constriction of the bronchioles, the tubes that take air to the lungs,
and make breathing more difficult. Drugs used to treat asthma
stimulate the processes that widen these tubes—most of the drugs
that asthmatics take stimulate the beta receptors for norepinephrine; beta receptors on the bronchioles widen these tubes, revers-
ing the symptoms of asthma—allowing easier breathing.

It's easy to see why use of these drugs by athletes could be
controversial. The temptation to improve performance at any
price is high, and these drugs can widen the bronchioles at least
slightly even in normal people. They can also stimulate heart rate,
release fatty acids from fat for energy, and increase circulation in
the muscles. All of these effects could probably improve performance a little bit, although the few good exercise studies that
have been done on normal people haven't shown much benefit.

Inhalers provide a safe, effective way to deliver these drugs
directly to the bronchioles, and drugs that are given this way are
allowed in most sports if a physician has certified that an athlete
has asthma.

Taken orally, these drugs are distributed throughout the body and therefore are more dangerous. They can stimulate the heart, dilate blood vessels leading to muscles and mobilize fat enough to provide some benefit during training or during an event, but the increase in heart rate is risky in competitive situations. Regular use of oral preparations of bronchodilators may also lead to the type of heart damage described above for ephedrine. Finally, these drugs can also overstimulate receptors in muscles, causing tremors that can interfere with fine motor control during competition. For all these reasons, oral but not inhaled bronchodilators are banned.

## Decongestants

Newspapers report rampant abuse of decongestants in the National Hockey League. Apparently, athletes have been taking several pills before a game to play better and more aggressively. This is perhaps one of the silliest misuses of stimulant medication currently in vogue, though probably less dangerous than the habits of years gone by when football players popped amphetamine pills before a big game.

There is no evidence that pseudoephedrine preparations improve performance in terms of endurance or strength. The perception that athletes can get "up" for a game by taking pseudoephedrine is based mainly on the jitteriness that's felt when high doses are taken. Nasal decongestants can increase alertness slightly, but they don't produce the sort of euphoria caused by cocaine or amphetamine. They also aren't addicting, but they can create intense anxiety.

Nasal decongestants work on the alpha receptor system of the SNS to cause constriction of blood vessels, especially in the skin and internal organs. Nasal congestion happens when allergens trigger release of histamine and other vasodilators. Decongestants don't block histamine effects, but they stimulate competing receptors for norepinephrine to constrict the smooth muscle surrounding the blood vessels. This counteracts the dilation caused by histamine and the other chemicals, helping to decrease the stuffy feeling.

They don't work miraculously in the nose only but on all small blood vessels throughout the body. Like asthma inhalers, nasal sprays that contain these compounds deliver the drug directly to the desired site of action and noplace else. Therefore they are not banned, nor should they be. However, the same drugs that are available as nasal sprays are also available as pills and syrups that are taken orally and distribute the drug throughout the body. They provide a more sustained delivery of drug to the desired site of action, constricting other blood vessels and raising blood pressure.

The big problem with the practice of taking pseudoephedrine before competing is that to get the alertness and jittery feeling, the athlete must take enough to risk a dangerous increase in blood pressure. Daily use can produce progressive, irreversible damage to the heart muscle. In the elderly, it can lead to enlargement of the prostate gland, resulting in difficulty urinating. All decongestants, not just banned decongestants, share these actions and dangers. Nasal sprays rarely cause these problems because they don't distribute drug throughout the body, and even the pills don't cause trouble when used occasionally for a stuffy nose. However, day-in, day-out use during training or competition offers little performance benefit and considerable risk.

## Caffeine

Caffeine seems perfect as a performance-enhancing drug: a safe and legal stimulant. Caffeine is used daily by most Americans, and it's taken seriously enough in the community of elite athletes that the American cycling team used it in the Olympics.

## DOES IT WORK? IS IT SAFE?

Caffeine is used throughout the world as a mild stimulant that increases arousal and mildly activates the SNS. Typical doses slightly increase blood pressure and heart rate. Caffeine also mildly dilates the bronchioles, making it easier for air to pass into the lungs. In fact, the chemical relative of caffeine called *theophylline* that we discussed earlier as a fat-melting cream was used widely in combination with ephedrine to treat asthma until the introduction of the more specific drugs. Caffeine also stimulates fat cells to release free fatty acids that can be used as an energy source. This is helpful during aerobic exercise because it promotes the use of stored fat, which is plentiful, instead of the stores of carbohydrates, which are less plentiful. For all these reasons, it would seem that caffeine would be ideal in long-term aerobic exercise like distance cycling. Indeed, these are the arenas in which it is often used.

## DOES CAFFEINE IMPROVE ATHLETIC PERFORMANCE?

Once again we enter the quagmire of trying to compare the average morning cup of coffee in sedentary office workers to "controlled laboratory studies" giving large doses of caffeine—generally in the range of three to four cups of coffee—to the megadoses chosen by some athletes. Even in regular coffee drinkers, caffeine produces a very small boost in blood pressure, heart rate, and alertness. Studies in well-trained athletes given reasonably large doses—two to three cups of coffee—are mixed. The general consensus is that performance of aerobic exercise can be improved. However, there are also some studies that do not show this effect, while still others showed improvements in exercise capacity only if caffeine was combined with ephedrine. Thus, while there is no question that caffeine has effects on the SNS, and on availability of nutrients in the bloodstream, the effects on physical performance are not so consistent. In the end, some investigators have concluded that caffeine, like amphetamine, may be most useful due to its ability to increase alertness.

Caffeine works a little differently from the other stimulants in

If you are a big coffee drinker, should you stop coffee for a few days before a major competition, then start again on the day of the event in order to realize a big improvement of performance? This has been suggested by some researchers. It's based on the fact that most coffee drinkers experience a headachy, tired feeling if they skip their morning coffee. This is a kind of withdrawal syndrome. Of course, if you feel lousy because you aren't getting coffee for a few days, a big jolt of caffeine on the day of competition is going to feel great. However, it's not clear that your performance would be any better than if you had just kept drinking coffee all along and had your normal cup of Joe on that day. In short, we don't really know if a brief withdrawal period really increases the performance-enhancing effects of caffeine, although caffeine does seem to work best in people who rarely use it.

this chapter. Although it does cause a mild stimulation of the sympathetic nervous system, it does not act directly on the neurons that use norepinephrine as their neurotransmitter. Instead, caffeine blocks receptors for the neurotransmitter *adenosine*. Adenosine slows down neural activity, so when caffeine prevents adenosine from doing its job, the brain is aroused. Adenosine also promotes fat deposition, so when caffeine prevents this action, it promotes the breakdown of fat. Finally, at high doses, caffeine can work directly in muscles to increase the release of calcium inside the muscle fiber. This release of calcium is one of the events that normally triggers muscle contraction, and so high doses of caffeine can cause muscle contractions. This is the one of bases of the tremors that many coffee users notice when they drink that third or fourth cup.

*WHAT ARE THE DANGERS OF CAFFEINE?*

An amount of caffeine equal to about thirty cups of coffee can be lethal. At tremendously high doses caffeine can increase the excitability of the nervous system so much that the person has seizures. It can also stimulate the SNS enough to cause disordered heart rhythms. At more modest doses (three to eight cups of coffee, depending on the person) caffeine can cause nausea, tremors, and sleeplessness. It is also a diuretic, which means that it increases urine production and loss of body water. This can be dangerous during prolonged exercise like cycling or distance running.

*WHAT ABOUT THE CONSEQUENCES OF LONG-TERM USE?*

The medical literature has gone back and forth on this issue. Since caffeine increases blood pressure, this is a concern in someone with cardiovascular disease. Yet most people who drink a daily cup or two of coffee don't experience more heart troubles, and most scientists estimate that under 500 milligrams per day of caffeine (about five cups of coffee) probably does not represent a significant long-term health risk. However, we don't know what happens to people who take the huge doses that some athletes do prior to or during competition. So we suggest caution.

## Tolerance to Stimulants

All of the stimulants listed above stop working if they are used continuously. In general, the body's receptor systems adapt to the excessive stimulation produced by most drugs by becoming less reactive to stimulation. This is true for all the stimulants, from amphetamine to pseudoephedrine. The extent of tolerance is determined by how much drug a person uses and by how long the use continues. Many athletes are savvy about this, and they develop training regimens designed to minimize the development of tolerance. Typically, they take the drug on alternate days or take one day on, two days off, etc.

## Blood Doping and EPO

The drugs listed above do their best to augment the normal systems by dilating the bronchioles, stimulating the cardiovascular system, and opening up blood flow to the muscles. But there are upper limits to the amount of air that can be inspired and the amount of blood that can be delivered to the muscles. To transcend these limits, athletes have shifted to the only other way to increase oxygen: increasing the number of red blood cells in the circulation, using two very different methods.

The first is called *blood doping*. The athlete removes blood (typically about 2 pints) several months before a big competition, freezes the red blood cells, then reinjects them just before the race. In the intervening months, the athlete's body has replaced the missing red blood cells, so the extra red blood cells allow the blood to carry more oxygen. In a normal man, about 40 percent of the blood volume is taken up by red blood cells. If you can increase that number by 10 or 20 percent, you can increase the oxygen-carrying capacity of the blood about perhaps as much as 10 to 15 percent. This is a huge increase, and it translates into increased exercise capacity during prolonged aerobic exercise.

Scandinavian endurance athletes (runners and cross-country skiers) first popularized this strategy during the early 1970s. Blood doping clearly conveys a performance advantage, and the practice spread like wildfire through the communities of endurance athletes (running, cross-country skiing, cycling). Blood doping was not banned until the late 1980s, in part because athletes argued that they should be allowed to use parts of their own bodies! Ultimately, safety considerations as well as ethical reasons led to its ban.

Recombinant DNA technology has improved on this process. The kidney normally produces a protein called *erythropoietin*, or EPO for short. EPO stimulates the production of new red blood cells. The use of recombinant DNA to mass produce this protein was a godsend for the many patients suffering from extreme anemias—diseases in which not enough red blood cells are produced. Unfortunately, it also simplified blood doping for athletes. Instead of messy transfusions and difficult storage problems, athletes could just get injections of EPO, then let their bodies produce even more red blood cells than is feasible to infuse through doping. EPO use has become so rampant in some sports that it is compromising their very integrity. For example, the 1998 Tour de France was struck by a scandal when several teams were caught with supplies of EPO, and the 1999 race ran under the same cloud.

Why do these two techniques work so well? Oxygen is carried from the lungs to the tissues that need it by binding to a molecule called hemoglobin inside red blood cells. If athletes have more red blood cells, their blood can carry more oxygen.

Despite the obvious advantages that blood doping and EPO may convey to a competitive athlete, there are also dangers. The greatest one is that much greater strain is placed on the heart by forcing it to pump a more viscous (i.e., "stickier") blood. Blood is normally a mixture of fluid and cells. With a greater percentage of cells, the blood actually gets "thicker" and is harder to pump through small capillaries where the exchange of oxygen takes place in tissues. Several competitive athletes have died because their heart simply couldn't pump against the increased force. There is just no defensible reason to use EPO or blood doping in sports. Unlike many other performance-boosting strategies, this one is based on sound science, but it is dangerous.

## The Bottom Line

1. All the stimulants have about the same effects: they can increase alertness, decrease appetite, facilitate mobilization of energy reserves, and stimulate the cardiovascular system.
2. Side effects depend on how well each drug enters the brain and how specific it is.

3. All the stimulants have cardiovascular side effects that can be dangerous to athletes using these drugs during training or performance.

4. Caffeine is a very mild stimulant and might work slightly for improving performance in endurance events.

5. *Blood doping is dangerous.*

Chapter 7

# CHILLING OUT

## Alcohol and Marijuana

### CONTENTS

**Understanding the Effects of Alcohol**

**Acute Effects**

*The Heart*

*The Lungs*

*The Brain*

*Specific Training Issues*

BODY TEMPERATURE

CALMING OR ACTIVATING EFFECTS OF VERY LOW DOSES

*Special Considerations for Young People*

EFFECTS ON LEARNING AND MEMORY

SEDATION OR SLEEPINESS

TOLERANCE

**Chronic Effects**

*The Heart and Other Muscles*

*The Lungs*

*The Brain*

**Understanding the Effects of Marijuana**

**Marijuana Smoke and the Lungs**

*continued on next page*

**Acute Effects**
*The Heart and Endurance*
*The Brain*
*Other Aspects of Physical Performance*
**Chronic Effects**
**The Bottom Line**

You can't watch a major sporting event on television without getting the message from the commercials that alcohol can improve your sex life, enhance your friendships, and impress your friends. The fact that manufacturers pay premium rates for advertising during sporting events is not accidental. Sporting events and sporting news attract the attention of young and active people, and most people do their heaviest drinking during adolescence and early adulthood (despite the legal drinking age in the United States). For some athletes, and in certain sports, drinking alcohol is associated with the camaraderie of the team—a part of celebrating victory, mourning defeat, or promoting a feeling of connection between team members. The experiences that athletes share off the field can be very meaningful, extending the sense of family that comes from the mutual experience of teamwork. But alcohol is a complex drug with a lot of different effects on the body, and used unwisely it can undermine the hard work that athletes put into their sports.

## Understanding the Effects of Alcohol

For many years the effects of alcohol were thought to be rather simple. It is a solvent, and at high concentrations it slows down or stops the activity of cells by simply disrupting the functions of the cell wall. But many of the effects of alcohol on the body occur at much lower doses and result from its effects on specific types of cells such as those in the brain. Finally, the effects of alcohol are complicated and can even seem contradictory. As anyone who has ever used alcohol knows, sometimes it acts as an "upper," making you feel giddy, excited, talkative; and sometimes it acts as a "downer," calming you or making you sleepy. How these effects will play out depends on the dose, the characteristics of the drinker, and, to some extent, the situation.

Each person brings his or her own cards to the table—almost everyone responds to alcohol a bit differently. Heredity plays a significant role in how people feel after drinking, their likelihood of becoming addicted to alcohol, even the rate at which their bodies eliminate alcohol. But heredity is just one of a number of factors. A person's age, drinking history, and body type can all influence one's response to alcohol.

## Acute Effects

Most people don't think of alcohol as the kind of drug that can kill you right away, by overdose. But each year, mostly on college campuses, people do die from alcohol overdose. High doses of alcohol can kill because alcohol directly suppresses breathing. High doses of alcohol can also impair coordination and judgment to the degree that people end up in accidents. Why should this matter to athletes? Because you don't perform well when your knee is blown out from a nasty fall, when your arm is broken in a fight, or when you're dead.

## THE HEART

Science has discovered that even a single dose of alcohol has many effects, some subtle and some powerful, on the heart. Alcohol makes the heart pump less efficiently, so less blood is delivered to other organs, including skeletal muscles (the ones responsible for physical movement and strength).

One particularly interesting study looked at the effects of a dose of alcohol (equal to 4–5 drinks) on heart function in young men at rest and during exercise. Those given alcohol achieved an average blood alcohol level of about 120 milligram percent (either 80 or 100 milligram percent is considered illegal for driving in the United States, depending on state laws); during exercise they showed bigger heart rate increases but smaller blood pressure rises than those who had no alcohol. This means that their hearts were working harder but distributing blood less effectively. After exercise it took four hours for heart rates to return to normal in the men who had alcohol, as opposed to one hour in the others. Clearly, the heart does not work as well during exercise, nor recover as quickly, in the presence of alcohol. Lower doses of alcohol, in the range of 30 to 100 milligram percent, seem to have similar effects.

In another study people were asked to rate how hard they were working while exercising. Alcohol did not influence most people's ratings, even though it caused their hearts to beat faster during the exercise session. This shows that sometimes a drug or other chemical can have powerful effects on the body without the individual being consciously aware of it. You aren't usually aware of your heart rate, blood pressure, and oxygen uptake, but all are essential to physical performance, and all are affected by alcohol.

## THE LUNGS

An overdose of alcohol can kill by suppressing breathing, but it does so by acting on the brain, not the lungs. Still, alcohol may have enough impact on the function of the lungs to concern athletes who rely on optimal lung function during training and competition. Alcohol suppresses reflexes in the upper airway that help to regulate the flow of air into and out of the lungs. Although this effect is mild at doses below about 100 milligram percent (the legal limit in a majority of U.S. states), any suppression will have an impact on airflow, particularly during exercise.

## THE BRAIN

The last thing an athlete wants is to decrease brain function. Jocks aren't dumb—they can't be if they really want to compete. You have to be sharp to meet the demands of training and competition. Without the brain, muscles wouldn't move on command, movements wouldn't coordinate into smooth sequences, and athletes couldn't absorb new information or learn new skills. Since the brain controls everything we do—physical and mental—any drug that affects it can change performance in many ways. Alcohol generally decreases the activity of brain cells, causing most functions to slow down and impairing most aspects of physical performance.

Although few people think it's valuable to train or compete while drunk, some people have thought that low doses might enhance performance. Because alcohol has a reputation for reducing anxiety (though the newest research says it does not), people sometimes think that using it might remove the jitters that come before competition. This is not so. More important, even low doses of alcohol impair complex physical functions like coordination and sequencing of movements. For example, although the legal limit for driving is 80 or 100 milligram percent, alcohol affects physical skills like those necessary for driving at much lower doses—in the range of 50 milligram percent (achieved in most people by about two drinks).

Alcohol is especially bad for your memory. While alcohol is in the bloodstream, people are less able to learn and store new information. This is because it inhibits activity in an area of the brain called the *hippocampus,* a region that is critical for the formation of new memories. Anyone who has ever been drunk has probably had the feeling that they don't have their usual clarity in remembering things that happened while drinking. This is because the brain is less able to turn information into memory with alcohol around. Many athletes spend long hours learning plays, remembering strategies, and thinking through the mental imagery of their performance. If their memories aren't working well, these efforts will pay fewer dividends.

So does this mean that all an athlete has to do is avoid drinking before a training film or strategy session? No. The way the brain creates memory is not that simple. It takes a long time for memories to form, and the brain is working hard to make them well after the person stops consciously "studying." The brain does a lot of its work later, while the person isn't thinking about the information. Some recent studies even show that some of the most important memory work happens during sleep, and we know that alcohol disrupts normal sleep patterns. So drinking in the evening, after a long day of studying in the library or film room, is probably bad timing for memory formation.

Another thing that happens during sleep is the release of

growth hormone, the body's internal signal to grow bigger and stronger—particularly important for athletes as part of the normal muscle-building and repair process. Because of its effects on sleep patterns, alcohol can decrease sleep-related growth hormone release by as much as 70 percent.


## SPECIFIC TRAINING ISSUES

*BODY TEMPERATURE*

Our bodies can only function normally when they are within a narrow range of temperatures. Since the temperature outside the body can change so much, we have evolved an elegant internal thermostat for keeping our body temperature stable. You can feel this thermostat at work when you sweat during exercise. The evaporating sweat cools your skin and lowers your temperature. Alcohol affects body temperature in two ways: by acting on the brain and by causing blood vessels near the skin to dilate. The brain effect impairs the body's ability to regulate its own temperature, and the effect on blood vessels causes a loss of body heat through the skin. During training, when body temperature rises as a result of exercise, these effects are magnified. Scientists used to think that alcohol only lowered body temperature because that's what happened in early studies. But alcohol actually impairs the ability of the body to regulate temperature in either direction. Contrary to popular beliefs about the effects of a cold beer in hot weather, alcohol causes an increase in body temperature when people drink it in hot environments. People have even died from drinking too much while sitting in hot tubs.

Since alcohol impairs temperature regulation, exercising with alcohol on board in hot or cold environments can be dangerous. A study of young men who exercised intermittently in a cold environment showed that even with low blood-alcohol levels, well below legal intoxication, they lost more heat during exercise. Alcohol may increase the chances of accidental hypothermia (dangerous loss of body temperature) during exercise in the cold.

Finally, don't be fooled by the old adage that alcohol helps keep the body warm in the cold, or by the image of a St. Bernard bounding through the Alps with a cask of brandy at its throat. People may feel warmer soon after a drink in the cold because alcohol dilates blood vessels near the skin. However, the effects of alcohol on temperature regulation will soon kick in, and the body will begin to lose heat.

### CALMING OR ACTIVATING EFFECTS OF VERY LOW DOSES

One of the most interesting things about alcohol is that its effects are *biphasic*—under some conditions it causes sedation or sleepiness, but under others it acts like a stimulant. People often describe a feeling of stimulation or activation with low doses that's replaced by sleepiness as they consume more alcohol. You may feel happy, talkative, and uninhibited soon after drinking, when the amount of alcohol in the blood is on the rise. But after the blood-alcohol level peaks and begins to head downward, often so do your feelings. With your blood-alcohol level falling, you are more likely to feel mellow, tired, or even a bit depressed.

Since low doses of alcohol can have activating effects, some people think that they might improve physical performance. Not much research exists on this, but according to what there is, this is not true. One study examined the effects of very low doses (1–10 milligrams per deciliter) on 5-mile run times in well-trained male runners, and found that their times were not enhanced by alcohol. In fact, though the difference was not statistically significant, their times tended to be somewhat worse on the higher of the two doses.

# SPECIAL CONSIDERATIONS FOR
# YOUNG PEOPLE

Alcohol can affect children, adolescents, and maybe even people in their early twenties differently than it does adults. It seems strange at first that the same drug would have such different effects at different ages. But neuroscience has taught us that the brain is actually continuing to develop and change as a person grows into his or her twenties, and the developing brain has unique sensitivities and vulnerabilities. So it makes sense that a drug that acts so strongly on the brain might have effects in adolescents that are dissimilar from those in adults. Most of the work on this topic has been done using experimental animals because it would be illegal and unethical to give alcohol to human adolescents in the laboratory. Yet the evidence is mounting that something very different happens when young mammals consume alcohol.

## EFFECTS ON LEARNING AND MEMORY

One of the best known effects of alcohol is that it impairs the ability to learn new information. Adolescents appear particularly vulnerable to this effect—it takes much less alcohol to impair memory in adolescent animals than in adults, and the brain changes that are necessary for learning are more easily disrupted by alcohol in adolescents. This may be true in humans, as well. In one study we found that a single dose of alcohol (below the legal limit for intoxication) had a much more powerful impact on learning in people twenty-one to twenty-four years of age than in those just a few years older, in their late twenties.

## SEDATION OR SLEEPINESS

On the other hand adolescents are *less* sensitive than adults to the sedative effects of alcohol. It takes much more alcohol to make adolescent animals fall asleep, and when they do, they wake up sooner and with more alcohol in their blood. Does this mean that it's safer for adolescents to drink and drive? Absolutely not! Just because a person isn't sleepy does *not* mean that he or she can drive well. Driving requires complex skills that are impaired by alcohol at doses well below those that would make a person feel sleepy. Likewise, just because someone still has the energy to go skiing or snowboarding or diving after a couple of drinks does *not* mean it's a good idea. In those cases, sleep would be a lot safer than complex physical activity requiring good reflexes and coordination.

TOLERANCE

The body adapts to some of the effects of alcohol over time. It takes higher doses to produce the same effects as before. This process, called *tolerance,* is one of the processes that contributes to addiction. Recent studies in animals show that certain forms of tolerance develop more rapidly in adolescents than in adults. If adolescents develop tolerance more quickly, they may be at greater risk for addiction. Indeed, studies show that people who begin drinking in their teens are much more likely to develop alcohol addiction problems than those who begin later in life. Clearly, a young athlete would not want to wander down a path that might lead to alcohol addiction.

# Chronic Effects

*Chronic drinking* does not just refer to decades of alcohol abuse. It can also describe a pattern of regular drinking over a relatively short period of time. For example, many college athletes may drink very little or not at all during the week, but drink a lot on the weekend or after a game. Many teams have a "no drinking in season" agreement, but have no policy about how much drinking goes on during the off season. Similarly, the forty-something weekday jogger might "reward" herself with three to four drinks on Friday and Saturday nights for a good week of workouts. This pattern may be worse for the body than spreading the same number of drinks more evenly across seven days because the brain can't adapt to the off-and-on stimulation of intermittent drinking. Everyone's drinking patterns are different, but if alcohol is a consistent part of the person's life for months or years, then it's worth thinking about the effects of "chronic" drinking.


## THE HEART AND OTHER MUSCLES

The press has touted the "protective" effect of drinking against heart disease. This does appear to be true for people who drink lightly—in the range of one drink per day—and is probably related to alcohol increasing high-density lipoproteins (HDLs, the so-called good cholesterol) in the blood. However, alcohol has other effects on the heart that are negative and can offset its protective effects, particularly at higher drinking levels.

Chronic, heavy drinking damages the heart muscle. One very detailed study of men who had been drinking for an average of sixteen years showed that their hearts pumped less effectively and demonstrated evidence of muscle damage. There was a direct relationship between the amount of alcohol they had consumed over the years and the weakness of their hearts. The more alcohol they had drunk, the weaker their heart muscles. But these men had not only suffered damage to their hearts. Their skeletal muscles were also weaker. Their deltoid (shoulder) muscles were weak and showed signs of damage. So after some years of relatively heavy drinking, both heart muscle and skeletal muscle are damaged—not a good outlook for anyone who hopes to maintain a healthy heart and an active physical lifestyle over the years.

## THE LUNGS

Chronic heavy drinkers are more prone to developing lung diseases, which could be related to lifestyle or drinking or both. One study that controlled for many lifestyle and health factors (including smoking) concluded that alcohol drinking alone did not have a significant influence on lung function. On the other hand, a study of people from ages twenty to ninety concluded that alcohol consumption above about four drinks per day accelerated an age-related decrease in lung function. So it seems safe to say that the lungs are probably not as vulnerable a target for alcohol as the heart, but heavy drinking does put them more at risk.

## THE BRAIN

Brain imaging techniques and tests of mental function can measure the effects of long-term alcohol drinking on the brain. Both show that chronic drinking impairs brain function, especially learning and memory. Some of alcohol's most lasting effects are on the hippocampus, the part of the brain that's important for memory formation. When the hippocampus is damaged, people lose much of their ability to store new memories. It's not clear how much alcohol, over what period of time, causes brain damage or memory deficits, but most evidence suggests that people who drink in the range of three or more drinks per day on average are at risk.

Brain regions related to physical movement are also impaired after chronic alcohol use. One of these is the cerebellum, a structure that is particularly important for the coordination of movements. Many roadside sobriety tests administered by police are designed to test the function of the cerebellum. Chronic use of alcohol can damage the cerebellum permanently. Again, the exact amount of alcohol necessary to create this damage is not clear, but beyond a couple of drinks per day is probably risky. For most athletes it's probably not worth risking any structure so critical for the coordination of movements.

## Understanding the Effects of Marijuana

Even though it's illegal, marijuana is one of the most popular psychoactive drugs in the United States, used by an amazing diversity of people, from elementary-school children to elderly cancer patients. Very few people believe that it could enhance physical performance, but it certainly has other effects (mostly negative) on the body, no matter whether you are a young, actively competing athlete, or a fifty-something "weekend warrior" trying to stay in shape. Like most drugs, marijuana has both acute and chronic effects. But before discussing the "drug effects" of marijuana, it's important to address the more general issue of smoking.

## Marijuana Smoke and the Lungs

When you smoke marijuana, you are taking over four hundred chemicals into your lungs. This chemical cocktail has many effects, including those of delta-9-tetrahydrocannabinol (THC, the main psychoactive chemical in the marijuana plant). By now it's clear to just about everybody that smoking anything is bad for the lungs, and marijuana is no exception. Comparing the risks of marijuana smoke to those of cigarette smoke is not so simple. First of all, the smokes are not the same. They both contain tar and a number of carcinogens, but the amounts differ. And the pot smoker generally takes more smoke into the lungs and keeps it there longer, allowing more time for the toxic agents (and the THC) to be absorbed. On the other hand, he usually smokes fewer cigarettes each day than a tobacco smoker.

One class of carcinogens found in tobacco cigarettes (polynuclear aromatic hydrocarbons) are found in 50 to 70 percent greater concentrations in marijuana smoke. Even though pot smokers generally smoke far fewer joints than tobacco smokers do cigarettes, the high concentration of these carcinogens in marijuana is a serious concern. A firm linkage between marijuana smoking and lung cancer has not yet been established, but one probably will be in the future. Already one study has suggested that a person who smokes one to three marijuana joints per day is likely to suffer lung damage comparable to someone who smokes about five tobacco cigarettes per day, and we know that damage to the DNA in lung cells—a possible early sign of cancer—can occur in marijuana smokers.

Cancer is not the only risk of smoking marijuana. People who smoke three to four joints per day are as likely to suffer from chronic bronchitis as people who smoke one pack of cigarettes per day, and the lungs of chronic marijuana smokers don't produce as much airflow as the lungs of nonsmokers. Obviously, these effects will impair athletic performance. On the other hand, such negative effects occur less frequently than in regular cigarette smokers.

The bottom line is some of the components of marijuana smoke can damage the lungs. How much it takes to cause damage is not clear, but even a small decrease in lung function could mean the difference between winning and losing in competitive athletics.

## *Acute Effects*

### THE HEART AND ENDURANCE

Even at low doses marijuana increases heart rate and seems to lower its pumping efficiency. These effects occur both at rest and during moderate exercise and can last for hours. One study of young men who exercised after smoking marijuana showed that marijuana increased the workload on the heart. The largest effect on heart rate was during recovery—increasing the time it took for the heart rate to return to normal. The story is pretty much the same when athletes work to exhaustion. Researchers in Quebec found that smoking marijuana just before exercise increased heart rate, and this increase persisted even as the athletes approached their maximum exercise capacity. In fact, fewer than half the people who smoked before exercising were able to match their usual maximum effort. These are all good reasons for athletes not to use marijuana. One study of athletes who had smoked pot found that most of them had quit for reasons related to their training such as "to keep my wind," "to not get tired," or "to perform better."

### THE BRAIN

Marijuana's most powerful effects are on the brain, causing a strong impact on sports performance. THC affects the brain by interacting with specific receptors on brain cells. The very existence of receptors for THC in our brains raises important questions about why they are there and what purpose they serve. The highest concentrations of THC receptors are in brain areas that are critical for learning new information (the hippocampus), coordinating movements (the cerebellum), and refining and controlling physical movements (the basal ganglia).

THC generally decreases activity in these brain areas. In the hippocampus, it powerfully disrupts the ability of those cells to change their activity patterns, a critical event for turning new information into memory. Learning is not just the ability to store facts in a conscious way. We also learn when we train our bodies or work to hone our reflexes. Though we may not think of this as learning, it clearly is, and it requires no less work by the brain than studying for a chemistry exam. A drug like marijuana that powerfully impairs learning may compromise training in ways that the user does not perceive.

Most people think that memory is formed pretty quickly, that at most it takes hours or perhaps days to store new information. Actually, most of the information we take in remains vulnerable even up to three years after it's initially "learned." If the information is not rehearsed internally, or if the learner gets a nasty knock to the head or takes a drug that disrupts synaptic plasticity, memories can be disturbed or even completely lost. Since memories are vulnerable for a long time after initial learning, it's probably not wise to spend a long Saturday afternoon studying and then go and get stoned that night. The information that you spent so much time loading into your brain by day could get pretty cloudy that night. It won't be completely lost, but it may not be stored as well. In the world of competitive academics—particularly in the life of the student athlete—it's probably best to avoid such losses of memory efficiency.

There's also something very important that most people don't know about marijuana. THC actually stays in the body for quite a while after smoking. Its effects on learning and other mental functions can last for a couple of days after just one joint, and small amounts of THC and its by-products can be detected for *weeks* after smoking, This means that if you smoke several times per week, there may be no time at which your thinking skills are completely normal. If a football player trying to learn his playbook or a lacrosse goalie trying to perfect her reflexes and reaction times are using marijuana, they will very likely get less out of training.

## OTHER ASPECTS OF PHYSICAL PERFORMANCE

THC also impairs the ability to stand steadily, decreases reaction time, and disrupts eye-hand coordination, all of which are important for athletic performance. This loss of coordination is the reason that some states conduct field tests for marijuana in automobile drivers who are driving erratically. These effects can last for several hours. If one adds alcohol to the THC, the effects are even worse and last far longer, even if the dose of alcohol was below the legal limit.

## Chronic Effects

The jury is still out on the question of chronic marijuana use and brain function. Some early studies that gave very high doses to animals over long periods of time suggested that there might be damage to some brain areas. But people don't use nearly as much as those animals got. Later studies using nonhuman primates and more likely doses failed to show the same kinds of damage. One recent study showed that realistic concentrations of THC decreased the survival of hippocampal neurons that were removed from the brain and grown in the laboratory. Though very well done, that study is also hard to interpret—putting THC onto growing brain cells in the laboratory doesn't simulate THC's effects on a person smoking pot. It is wise to interpret such findings cautiously.

What about the long-term effects of marijuana on thinking and memory? These are among the most noticeable consequences of acute exposure, and there has been a lot of discussion about long-term marijuana smokers losing their memory capacity over time. Although science has not yet answered this question, the available evidence suggests that there is impairment, but only after a long period of heavy smoking.

For example, one study assessed memory and other mental functions in two groups of men. One group was in their midforties at the time of testing, and the other group was in their late twenties. Both age groups included some men who had smoked pot regularly and some who had not. The smokers in the younger group had been smoking for an average of eight years at a rate of about four joints, two to seven times per week. The men in the older group had been smoking for an average of thirty-four years at a rate of about five joints, two to seven times per week. The older men who had smoked regularly were slower to form new memories. They were also less able to engage in different ways of thinking in order to solve problems—a sign of mental inflexibility. The two groups of nonusers, and the group of younger users all performed about the same. This study suggests that it takes a lot of marijuana over a very long period of time to cause permanent deficits in mental functions.

Buried in this experiment is an unanswered question that may be very important. The older group of smokers used more marijuana over a longer period of time than the younger group, but *they also started using it much earlier in life,* around the age of twelve. The younger users' group didn't start until about the age of twenty. Could it be that the older group had cognitive deficits because they used marijuana while their brains were still developing, during adolescence?

Marijuana, like alcohol, may be particularly bad for the adolescent brain. People who start using marijuana between the ages of twelve and sixteen are significantly slower to react to visual information than those who start using after age sixteen or those who don't use marijuana. It may be that the earlier a person starts using pot, the more likely he or she will end up with deficits in the ability to process visual information.

These results may be related to how the visual system matures. Between the ages of twelve and fifteen the rate at which people are able to process visual information speeds up considerably. Marijuana affects this same kind of visual processing. So it may be that impairing this brain function with THC during the critical adolescent years alters the course of its development and leads to long-term deficits in visual function. This should be a sobering thought to young athletes who hope to use their visual reaction times to hit a curve ball, see a receiver come open, or block a soccer shot. Moreover, if this is true for visual processing, what about other brain functions that are still developing in adolescence? Might they also be impaired? We don't know because the research hasn't been done—but it's a plausible and disturbing possibility.

## The Bottom Line

1. Single doses of alcohol do not improve physical performance and create some risks.

2. High doses can kill you by suppressing breathing. Low doses can impair coordination of movements, the ability to learn new information, and regulation of your body temperature.
3. Long-term alcohol use damages both the heart and skeletal muscles. Mild alcohol use likely protects against heart disease, but after more than one drink per day the bad effects outweigh the good.
4. Alcohol has differing effects in people of different ages. In young people it impairs memory more but causes less sedation.
5. Smoking anything, including marijuana, is bad for the lungs. Chronic marijuana smoking may increase the risk of lung diseases.
6. Marijuana increases the heart's rate and workload during exercise and prolongs the heart's recovery afterward. It also decreases your maximum work capacity during hard exercise.
7. Marijuana impairs learning, memory, and other mental functions, and these effects persist long after the feeling of being high is gone—up to two days.
8. It takes a lot of marijuana use over a long period of time to produce permanent deficits in mental function in adults.
9. When marijuana use begins early, before the age of sixteen, it appears more likely to result in enduring problems related to visual and cognitive function.

Chapter 8

# SMOKING AND CHEWING

*Tobacco*

## CONTENTS

Nicotine: A Powerful Drug

Smokeless Tobacco

    *Effects on the Heart and Circulatory System*

    *Effects on Concentration, Reaction Time, and Strength*

    *Physical Performance and Health Consequences after*
        *Long-Term Use*

Nicotine Patches and Gum

Smoking

The Bottom Line

Tobacco use by humans has a long and eventful history. Native Americans used it as a ceremonial symbol of goodwill and as a medicine, and they introduced it to Christopher Columbus in 1492. In the sixteenth and seventeenth centuries many physicians considered it a virtual cure-all and used it to treat a wide variety of maladies. During the 1800s, well before smoking became popular, most tobacco factories produced chewing tobacco. Eventually, cigars and then cigarettes became popular. Now, cigars and smokeless tobacco have made a resurgence, but a striking number of people continue to smoke cigarettes.

## Nicotine: A Powerful Drug

Nicotine, the active ingredient in tobacco, was isolated and named by French chemists in 1828, who considered it a medicine. Nicotine affects the body many ways, but its most powerful effects are in the sympathetic nervous system (SNS) and the brain. Nicotine stimulation of the SNS increases the heart rate and the workload on the heart. It also constricts blood vessels, raises blood pressure, and compromises circulation in some areas. These effects diminish the heart's pumping efficiency and can compromise athletic performance.

Nicotine affects the brain in two main ways. It enhances concentration, and it is addictive. Most athletes and physically active people think of themselves as strong, independent, and in control of their bodies. Addiction doesn't seem a likely path for them. But nicotine is a tricky drug. It's addictive without giving the user a distinctive "high." Few people report any kind of euphoria or "rush" when using nicotine, and yet it powerfully activates the reward systems in the brain, leading to the urge to use the drug again. People also become tolerant to the effects of nicotine so that they are likely to increase their usage as they develop the habit. Unpleasant withdrawal symptoms occur when a chronic user quits, and although these are relatively short-lived, they can make quitting very difficult. All of these effects—activating the brain's reward system, promoting tolerance, and withdrawal—are part of the addictive process and are produced by any kind of tobacco use, not just cigarettes.

Nicotine addiction is one of the reasons that nicotine has resurfaced as a medicine. Smoking cessation programs use controlled doses to help people kick the habit. How could a drug be used to treat addiction to itself? The answer lies in how it's administered. Most people who seek treatment for addiction to nicotine became addicted by smoking. When a drug is smoked, it's absorbed into the blood and passed to the brain very rapidly. This rapid loading of the brain is a setup for the addiction process. But when nicotine gum or skin patches are used, the drug doesn't hit the brain as quickly. Even though the brain may get as much nicotine from these sources as from cigarettes, the way it gets there makes addiction less likely. During the first six to twelve weeks after giving up cigarettes, this kind of smoother exposure to nicotine can help curb the urge to smoke without placing the person at additional risk for addiction.

Fortunately most athletes and other physically active people don't smoke cigarettes, but many do use smokeless tobacco. Also, the rising popularity of cigars indicates that more and more people are consuming considerable amounts of nicotine even though they don't inhale.

## Smokeless Tobacco

Smokeless tobacco is placed in the mouth—a very good site for drug absorption due to its rich blood supply. The tissues that line the inside of the mouth are also rather thin compared with other body barriers such as the skin, making it easier for chemicals to cross into the blood. In some sports—most notably baseball and football, though others are catching up—the use of smokeless tobacco has become a part of the culture of the sport. Many athletes believe that nicotine enhances their concentration and improves their reaction times. They also view smokeless tobacco as safe. Both of these beliefs are wrong.

*Leaf tobacco*, or "chewing tobacco," is generally sold in pouches, and the leaf is placed in the mouth between the inside of the cheek and lower gum. The small ball of tobacco is then gently chewed or sucked, and saliva is generally spit out. *Snuff* is another popular form of smokeless tobacco. It may be either moist or dry, but the tobacco is in powder form—not the longer, shredded leaf form of chewing tobacco. Snuff is generally sold in small round cans, and a small pinch is placed between the cheek or lip and the lower gum. This is often called "dipping." The third popular form of smokeless tobacco is *compressed tobacco*. This is simply leaf tobacco that's compressed into a firm brick. A small piece, called a "plug," is bitten or cut off the brick and placed in the mouth between the lip or cheek and lower gum, as in dipping.

Smokeless tobacco results in about the same peak blood nicotine level as smoking a cigarette, but since the oral tobacco lasts longer, it delivers a lot more nicotine over a longer time frame, and the effects of the nicotine last much longer.

## EFFECTS ON THE HEART AND CIRCULATORY SYSTEM

Despite the mystique surrounding smokeless tobacco, the effects of nicotine on the heart tend to impair physical performance, not enhance it. Nicotine increases resting heart rate and blood pressure, creating extra work for the heart. It can lower the pumping efficiency of the heart during exercise up to 25 percent, according to one study. Nicotine also reduces the efficiency with which the cardiovascular system supplies blood to muscles and other body tissues.

There have been a number of good studies of the effects of smokeless tobacco on heart function both at rest and during exercise. One particularly detailed study assessed the effects of smokeless tobacco use while at rest and during various levels of exercise, in healthy young men who were already users of smokeless tobacco. The researchers wanted to know about the effects of smokeless tobacco on oxygen uptake, the volume of blood pumped by the heart, and the speed with which lactate accumulates in the blood with exercise (a biochemical measure that relates to muscle fatigue and endurance). The subjects were given either snuff or a placebo "dip," then exercised on a graded treadmill task through increasing stages of difficulty to exhaustion. Nicotine increased heart rate at all levels until the heart rate reached its maximal exercise level, probably because the heart rate was approaching its physiological "ceiling." Although heart rate increased, the amount of blood pumped with each heart beat decreased after nicotine. So smokeless tobacco increases the work that the heart has to do to supply other body tissues, including muscles. Nicotine also increased the accumulation of lactate in the blood during exercise, particularly during submaximal exercise. This means that with nicotine on board, the subjects were probably depleting energy stores more rapidly and might be expected to experience muscle fatigue sooner. This could diminish endurance.

The jury is still out on the ultimate question of whether nicotine actually impairs endurance or the capacity for physical work. But it is fair to say that, regardless of how it's delivered, nicotine causes the heart to work harder and less efficiently both at rest and during exercise. This can't be a good thing for the competitive athlete looking for an edge, and it might actually be dangerous for the weekend warrior pushing for a maximal cardiovascular workout.

## EFFECTS ON CONCENTRATION, REACTION TIME, AND STRENGTH

Athletes use smokeless tobacco for two main reasons. First, they believe that the nicotine gives them a competitive edge by increasing their ability to concentrate and thus improve their reaction times. Second, smokeless tobacco has become very deeply engrained in the culture of certain sports. A survey of male college athletes in the early 1990s showed that 57 percent of baseball players, 40 percent of football players, and 20 percent of track-and-field athletes used smokeless tobacco. And the use wasn't restricted to men. Among women athletes, 9 percent of softball players and 5 percent of track-and-field athletes reported using smokeless tobacco. It is very unlikely that so many athletes would use it if they did not believe that it gave them a competitive edge. Still, the scientific literature indicates that it probably does not.

When college-age men were tested for reaction time, the time it takes to complete a movement, and the ability to visually track an object, smokeless tobacco caused no improvements. This was true for both athletes and nonathletes, though the athletes did have faster reaction times in general. Smokeless tobacco also proved ineffective in more real-world situations for athletes, such as visually tracking a moving object and anticipating its end position, or reacting as quickly as possible to a flash of light while making a decision about the direction from which it came.

In fact, smokeless tobacco use may worsen performance. In one experiment it decreased the maximum force that could be generated in a knee extension during a simple reaction-time test. And when the subjects had to make decisions about stimuli in the environment during the test, tobacco also decreased the speed with which the force could be generated—decreasing the power of the movement.

## PHYSICAL PERFORMANCE AND HEALTH CONSEQUENCES AFTER LONG-TERM USE

Although many people think of smokeless tobacco as a safe alternative to smoking, long-term use significantly increases the risk of deadly oral cancer. Unfortunately, many young people (and athletes are no exception) simply don't look very far into the future with respect to their health. The promise of getting a performance edge *now* (regardless of how hollow that promise may be) can easily outweigh statistics about increased disease risks years down the road. A sense of perspective can be very important, and coaches can have a great impact by helping young athletes to understand it and make healthy long-term decisions.

A long list of diseases of the mouth are prevalent in chronic users of smokeless tobacco. Smokeless tobacco users have nearly two and a half times as many dental cavities as nonusers, in part because both leaf and plug tobacco preparations contain high concentrations of sugar (about 20 to 35 percent). But cavities may be the least of the users' concerns. Gum recession is common with chronic use, often leading to periodontal disease involving bone and tooth loss. One study found these types of degeneration already occurring among high school students who had used smokeless tobacco for about three hours per day on average. The delicate inner lining of the cheeks and mouth can also become diseased; a study found "soft tissue lesions" in 49 percent of high school users. One particularly ominous soft tissue lesion common to the mouths of smokeless tobacco users is called *leukoplakia*. This looks like a white patch or plaque, and it can be precancerous.

The incidence of oral cancers is much higher in longtime smokeless tobacco users than in the general public. Baseball player Brett Butler experienced a type of oral cancer that is very common in smokeless tobacco users, even though he stopped using smokeless tobacco fifteen years before he developed cancer. Unfortunately, cancers can take years to develop, and his experience is all too common. Because of his cancer, Mr. Butler now cautions other athletes about the use of smokeless tobacco.

## Nicotine Patches and Gum

Patches and gum are mostly used to help people quit smoking, and they have been found to be very helpful when used in conjunction with other strategies such as behavioral therapy, relaxation, and emotional support. When used as directed, these methods are safe and don't deliver excessive amounts of nicotine, generally no more than a heavy smoker would take in over the course of a day.

Since nicotine gum is seldom used as an aid to physical performance, there's simply not much research on the topic. But there is no reason to think that nicotine gum or patches will be of any more help than smokeless tobacco, which provides no benefit. The amount of nicotine released by the patch may increase by 13 to 30 percent during exercise, depending upon the particular patch being used, which could be risky for people with heart problems. It is always wise to consult with one's physician before using a patch or nicotine gum.

## Smoking

*Don't smoke.* The nicotine won't help physical performance, the carbon monoxide in combination with the nicotine will damage your heart, and the carcinogens in the smoke will dramatically increase your risk of lung cancer.

Fortunately most athletes and physically active people don't need a lecture about all the negative health consequences of smoking. But it's worthwhile to know that although most people think of lung cancer as the primary killer associated with cigarette smoking, heart disease is responsible for many more deaths, and it has been estimated that as many as 30 percent of deaths attributed to heart and vascular disease are related to smoking.

As for physical and sports performance, smoking is exclusively bad news. Smoking makes the heart work less efficiently because of the combined effects of nicotine and carbon monoxide. Chronic smoking also reduces one's oxygen uptake and maximum workload during exercise. Essentially, smoking works against most of the effort that athletes put into their training.

Smoking also effects another aspect of physical performance that may be of interest, particularly to men. It markedly increases the incidence of erectile dysfunction (i.e., impotence). A study of over four thousand men, from thirty-one to forty-nine years of age showed that smokers were 50 percent more likely to have problems with achieving or maintaining erections. This was the case even when controlling for a raft of other social and medical factors that could contribute to erectile dysfunction. In other words, smoking by itself is a significant risk factor for erectile dysfunction among men in this relatively young age range.

## The Bottom Line

1. Smoking tobacco harms athletic performance through its effects on lung and cardiovascular function.
2. Nicotine does not improve reaction times, reflexes, or the ability to make rapid and accurate choices. Nicotine may actually impair performance because of adverse effects on heart function and muscular power.
3. Smokeless tobacco is not a safe alternative to smoking nor does it improve athletic performance. Chronic use of smokeless tobacco increases the risks of various cancers as well as other serious dental and oral diseases.

## Chapter 9

# COOLING DOWN

### CONTENTS

Valium and Other Sedative/Hypnotics

*Natural Sedation? Kava Kava*

GHB and GBL

Narcotic Painkillers

Natural Opiates: Endorphins, Runner's High, and
  Amenorrhea

Beta Blockers

Prozac and Its Friends

  *Appropriate Use of Antidepressants*

The Bottom Line

E thanol—the active ingredient in alcoholic beverages—is the sedative most often used by athletes. In our culture, alcohol isn't really considered to be a drug but rather a beverage, a social convention and a tool for social interaction. The intentional use of sedative or calming drugs by athletes is much more unusual because most athletes have the sense to understand that slowing down the brain is likely to hurt, not help, performance. Sedative drugs are designed to gradually slow the activity of all the neural centers in the brain. Usually the goal is to decrease anxiety or make a person sleepy. However, these drugs are very nonspecific, and they slow down the centers involved in controlling movement as well as interfere with training by impairing learning and memory. Still, there are a few circumstances in which athletes will encounter sedative or depressant drugs or, even more rarely, will consider using them to enhance performance.

## Valium and Other Sedative/Hypnotics

Athletes get anxious before big meets and have trouble sleeping. On rare occasions this can lead to the temptation to use sedative or anxiety-reducing drugs. Drugs like diazepam (Valium) or alprazolam (Xanax) are currently the drugs of choice to medically treat anxiety disorders. These drugs are much safer than older style sedatives like barbiturates because they decrease anxiety and cause some sedation, but they're almost never lethal with an overdose. An occasional single dose isn't likely to cause any trouble. Mixing these drugs with alcohol is another story, however, and a lethal combination. The combined dose is far more dangerous than either drug separately. Rohypnol ("roofies"), the famous "date-rape" drug, is really just a benzodiazepine-type drug that is effective in small doses, takes effect very quickly, and at sedative doses—especially in combination with alcohol—can cause unconsciousness and amnesia.

On a performance level, these drugs are muscle relaxants and mild sedatives. They increase reaction time and impair coordination. Therefore, whenever they are present in the bloodstream, they can impair performance. Since most of these drugs were designed to decrease anxiety all day long for people with anxiety disorders, most are still in the bloodstream the next morning, producing a little bit of drowsiness and a hungover feeling that nobody wants on race day. A few newer drugs, including Halcion (triazolam) and Ambien (zolpidem), have been developed that get around this problem because they act in the same way as diazepam but have a much shorter duration of action. These drugs are basically gone in a few hours, so you don't have the hungover feeling the next day. However, the sleep that you get when you take these drugs (like the sleep you get after drinking) is not normal sleep. You spend much less time in the most restful stage of sleep, the one that causes deep muscle relaxation. Taking one of these pills may be better than not sleeping at all, but it certainly isn't as good as a normal night's sleep.

It's important to remember that the effects of these drugs can outlast the time that one can feel them. A highly trained and skilled athlete may lose her "edge" for many hours after the major sedative effects have disappeared. Basically, no drug that reduces anxiety or produces sedation does not impair athletic performance. If you must use these drugs, give them a few days to clear your body before you need to have peak performance.

## Natural Sedation? Kava Kava

Kava kava is a natural product that is being touted widely as a "safe and natural" sedative. This is probably just an example of the never-ending resourcefulness of human beings at finding intoxicants—and the sluggish way the bureaucracies respond to social change. Kava kava is a plant that is made into a beverage in the South Pacific, where it is an important focus of social life. Kava kava is used and abused there much in the way that alcohol is in this country. At reasonable doses, it is a mild sedative/hypnotic. However, some people use it habitually in high doses and experience many of the same problems that alcoholics experience. The active compounds have been identified, and the way kava kava causes sedation and sleep is probably the same as alcohol. So this is not a magic organic sleep aid that works in some novel way. It likely has the same drawbacks as alcohol. Furthermore, the actions of these compounds are quite complicated, and there are some known toxicities (a scaly skin rash and liver and kidney damage) that result from long-term use. People who have abused kava kava for a long time have had very significant and permanent cardiovascular damage.

## GHB and GBL

Gamma-hydroxybutyrate (GHB) and its precursor gamma-butyrolactone (GBL) are popular on the party circuit because they are easy and cheap to make. GHB causes sedation, much like alcohol. GBL is turned into GHB in the body, and so it has the same effects. Like other sedatives, GHB can be deadly. It is possible to die from a single dose if it is too large. Unfortunately, virtually all of the GHB that's readily available is homemade, and usually only the person who made it really knows the dose. GHB occurs naturally in the body and has been implicated in hibernation and other natural states of sedation. There are receptor molecules in the brain for GHB. However, we have very little idea how this drug works or what it really does to normal brain function. It has been used as a medicine in Europe to treat narcolepsy (a sleep disorder) and as an anesthetic, and it has been shown to induce a state resembling petit mal epilepsy. At the doses that people take recreationally, it acts like alcohol. Higher doses can cause seizures, decreases in breathing, and coma. Overdoses, including deaths, are more and more common as GHB popularity continues to rise on the party circuit.

GHB and GBL have double lives: party drugs and food supplements. Health-food stores and supplement marketers advertise GHB and GBL aggressively in many forms: 2(3H)-furanone dihydro; butyrolactone; gamma-butyrolactone; 4-butyrolactone; dihydro-2(3H)-furanone; 4-butanolide; 2(3H)-furanone, dihydro; tetrahydro-2-furanone; and butyrolactone gamma, to name a few. They are marketed most recently as safe and natural sleep aids and occasionally as anabolic agents.

However, there is just no good reason to use GHB or GBL. These drugs are ineffective as anabolic agents and dangerous as sedatives. Just recently, media reports said that NBA player Tom Gugliota experienced a seizure while taking GHB as a "natural" supplement to promote sleep. He was likely completely unaware of the drug's danger—and is fortunate that he escaped unscathed.

## Narcotic Painkillers

Mankind has used the drugs derived from the opium poppy probably for thousands of years. The compounds in the opium poppy, called *narcotic analgesics*, are the most effective painkillers that exist. Codeine and morphine are compounds found naturally in the opium poppy, while heroin is a slight modification of morphine. There have been some modern improvements in the structure (meperidine and fentanyl are a couple that are well-known), but the basic action of all of these drugs is the same. However, they vary widely in how great an effect they produce. Heroin, morphine, meperidine (Demerol) and fentanyl are strong narcotics that can easily kill in overdose but can provide excellent pain relief after surgery. Oxycodone and codeine are weaker opiates that are often prescribed in pill form after surgery, but these provide less pain relief. Narcotic analgesics were among the first drugs abused by European athletes, when in early bicycle races they were included in cocktails that were supposed to improve performance.

Narcotic analgesics do nothing to the cause of pain, but they diminish the ability of pain impulses to get to the brain, and they also decrease the perception of a painful feeling as unpleasant. Instead, they induce a dreamy, sleepy, almost euphoric feeling. People who take these drugs say that they still experience pain, but it doesn't bother them.

Almost all narcotic analgesics except the weakest (codeine) are banned in high-level athletic competitions. Competing on painkillers obviously gives an unfair advantage to an athlete who wants to compete pain free, but it also puts the athlete at risk for further injury because the user ignores signs that something is wrong.

This doesn't mean that athletes should never take narcotic analgesics. Narcotic analgesics are ideal painkillers after minor surgery: many athletes receive fairly strong narcotics in the hospital immediately after surgery, plus prescriptions for weaker opiates when they go home. Athletes need to realize that while taking them, they will be much less alert than normal.

Using opiates during training or competition also doesn't make much sense because their other effects on the body impair performance. In addition to decreasing the feeling of pain, opiates decrease the rate of breathing, which athletes certainly don't want. They mildly depress the SNS and can make it harder for the brain to activate the cardiovascular system during exercise. While they are not sedative in the same way as Valium, they induce a sort of dreamy "don't care about anything state" that certainly is the opposite of the mental state that athletes want to experience. They are also constipating, which actually would be desirable in circumstances when athletes are experiencing a poorly timed attack of diarrhea. However, in general, they aren't going to do anything to improve athletic performance and will likely impair it.

With long-term use, opiates are definitely bad news. Addiction is a real risk, and people typically pay less attention to their nutrition, so they lose weight. Narcotics decrease immune function and so increase susceptibility to infections. Finally, narcotics taken regularly can impair reproductive function and prevent menstrual cycles. This is already a risk in a woman athlete who is training intensively. However, such effects are most typically seen in addicts who are using heavily, with a pattern of use that is likely incompatible with training, anyway.

Why do the rules of competition allow athletes to use nonsteroidal anti-inflammatory drugs like aspirin, acetaminophen, or ibuprofen but not narcotics? Aspirin, ibuoprofen, and similar drugs decrease the sensation of pain and can decrease inflammation, but they differ in very significant ways from opiates. First, they are much safer. Narcotic analgesics can kill you. With a single dose they can suppress the brain to the point that the person simply stops breathing. Second, all narcotic analgesics are addicting, ibuprofen is not. Furthermore, there is a limit to how well the nonsteroidal anti-inflammatory drugs work, and this reduces the chance that an athlete can ignore the pain and go on to experience much more severe injury. Basically, the culture of sports has accepted aspirin, ibuprofen, and its cousins because these drugs are so safe (and so ubiquitous). Nevertheless, any athlete should be careful to consider the potential for serious injury when using any drug to mask pain while training or competing.

## Natural Opiates: Endorphins, Runner's High, and Amenorrhea

Narcotic analgesic drugs work because they stimulate a receptor for compounds that our own brains produce, called *enkephalins* and *endorphins*. These molecules are neurochemicals that regulate the same functions that we manipulate with narcotics. Enkephalins regulate breathing, help modify the perception of pain, affect how the GI tract works, and do all the things that narcotic drugs do. The endorphin neurons are even more interesting. They exist in only a few places in the brain and are activated under very stressful circumstances. Scientists think that when extreme stress activates endorphin neurons, they induce a state of calm and lack of pain that allows the animal or person to face imminent disaster with tranquility.

Many people attribute "runner's high" to release of endorphins in the brain, and this may actually be correct. "Runner's high" is a near mystical state that can accompany the end of a marathon or similarly stressful endurance event. It is a state of near euphoria in which the exhaustion and pain are swept away by a feeling of peace, elation, and lack of pain that is actually pleasant. Extreme stress does activate endorphin neurons in animals, but there are only two sure ways to know this is true in people. The first is to take a sample of cerebrospinal fluid at the beginning and end of a race and measure endorphins—though obviously, not too many people are going to line up for *this* experiment! Theoretically it would be possible to treat people with a drug called naloxone (Narcan) that blocks the actions of endorphins, to see if it also blocks "runners high." As far as we know, this hasn't been tried yet.

Endorphins released during running may well be responsible in part for the loss of menstruation in women who are training too hard. One of the normal effects of endorphins is to decrease the release of the hormones that control the ovaries. If the endorphin neurons are activated too much, they decrease these hormones to the point that the athlete can't ovulate. This may just be part of the story, but the ability of the opiate blocker Narcan (mentioned above) to restore cycles in overtraining athletes lends credence to this possibility.

## Beta Blockers

Some athletes also use drugs that prevent some actions of the sympathetic nervous system. Since marked activation of the SNS creates the jittery, anxious feeling, palpitations, and tremor that happen naturally whenever we are anxious about something—the feeling of "stage fright" that many musicians, actors, and other performers experience—some athletes who experience these same feelings as the SNS prepares their bodies for exercise take a drug that can block the effects of adrenaline (epinephrine) and decrease the feelings of stage fright.

Drugs that block the beta receptor for norepinephrine and epinephrine prevent the heart pounding, palm sweating, and peripheral manifestations of the stress response that can be a real drawback in a sport like shooting or archery that requires calm composure and fine-motor coordination. Just eliminating these physical reactions can go a long way toward calming a performer or athlete. One of these drugs, propranolol, also enters the brain and can actually help soothe some of the anxious feelings as well. Other beta-blockers like atenolol just calm the peripheral effects because they don't get into the brain.

Beta-blockers are illegal in athletic competition for obvious reasons: gaining control over these feelings is part of the mastery of sport, and using drugs gives an unfair advantage to people who take them. Furthermore, there are some associated hazards. If the activity involved requires high levels of physical activity (like the biatholon), then the beta-blockers will prevent many of the needed adjustments the body makes during exercise: heart rate can't speed up, blood vessels to the muscles can't adapt to the work load, and bronchioles might constrict instead of dilating.

## Prozac and Its Friends

One group of antidepressants called *serotonin specific uptake inhibitors*, or SSRIs, have become popular in some sports like professional golf. Fluoxetine (Prozac), Zoloft (sertraline), and Paxil (paroxetine) are SSRIs. They increase the amount of serotonin available to receptors in much the same way that cocaine does. However, they act specifically on serotonin and so are useful for treating depression and some other mood disorders, but they are not addictive or dangerous in any way. Athletes say that they produce a feeling of calm that allows them to focus on the game. In this sense, their use resembles the use of beta-blockers. But the target here is the brain, and the feelings associated with competition. While these drugs are effective at treating mood disorders, there is no scientific evidence that they do any particular good for an already healthy brain.

## APPROPRIATE USE OF ANTIDEPRESSANTS

Athletes can get depressed just like anyone else, and then they may need treatment with antidepressants. Furthermore, overtraining like that typical in distance running and swimming can lead to a syndrome of exhaustion and low mood that might resemble depression. Injuries that take an athlete out of competition, or even end careers, can trigger depressive episodes that require treatment. Treatment of anorexic or bulimic athletes who are experiencing stress fractures, for example, can also include SSRIs, which can help with disordered eating behavior. Depression is life threatening. It is critical for athletes to get treatment like anyone else who is seriously depressed.

## *The Bottom Line*

1. All sedative and anxiety-reducing drugs impair coordination and disrupt sleep and memory formation. Natural sedatives are no better than synthetic ones.
2. Narcotic analgesics are important in treatment of pain after surgery or in limited circumstances, but they are illegal in most competitions, impair performance, and present some particular risks to athletes.
3. Athletes who have mood disorders need treatment like anybody else, and nobody should ever avoid treatment for depression.

# BIBLIOGRAPHY

*NOTE* This bibliography cites some general reference texts and recent scientific literature that address key points in *Pumped*. It is by no means exhaustive. If you read the citations carefully, you will see that it is difficult to find scientific studies that meet all the criteria we raised in Chapter 2 (How to Read the Ads). We have tried to list the best available studies supporting or refuting the effectiveness of various performance-enhancing agents. Nonetheless, many of these use small populations or populations like the elderly that are not relevant to the young, highly trained athlete. The first section gives textbooks and general reference books, and review articles. Scientific articles are listed chapter by chapter.

## General Reference Texts and Reviews

Bloch, A. S., and Shils, M. E. *Nutrition Facts Manual: A Quick Reference.* Baltimore, Md.: Williams and Wilkins, 1996.

Brick, J., and Erickson, C. *Drugs, the Brain, and Behavior: The Pharmacology of Abuse and Dependence*. Binghamton, N.Y.: The Hayworth Medical Press, 1998.

Catlin, T. H. Muarry. "Performance-Enhancing Drugs, Fair Competition and Olympic Sport." *Journal of the American Medical Association* 276 (1996): 231–237.

Clarkson, P. M. "Nutrition for Improved Sports Performance: Current Issues on Ergogenic Aids." *Sports Medicine* 6 (1996): 393–401.

Kreider, R. B. "Dietary Supplements and the Promotion of Muscle Growth with Resistance Exercise." *Sports Medicine* 27 (1999): 97-110.

Kuhn, C., Swartzwelder, H. S., and Wilson, W. A. *Buzzed: The Straight Facts About the Most Used and Abused Drugs from Alcohol to Ecstasy*. New York: W. W. Norton, 1998.

Laure, P. "Epidemiologic Approach to Doping in Sport." *Journal of Sports Medicine and Physical Fitness*. 37 (1997): 218-224.

McArdle, W. D., Katch, F. I., and Katch, V. L., *Exercise Physiology: Energy, Nutrition and Human Performance*. Baltimore, Md.: Williams and Wilkins, 1996.

Regan, T. "Alcohol and the Cardiovascular System." *Journal of the American Medical Association* 264 (1990): 377–381.

U.S. Department of Health and Human Services. Ninth Special Report to the U.S. Congress on Alcohol and Health. 1997.

Wagner, J. "Abuse of Drugs Used to Enhance Athletic Performance." *American Journal of Hospital Pharmacy* 46 (1989): 2059–2067.

Williams, M. H. "Nutritional Ergogenics in Athletics." *Journal of Sports Sciences* 13 (1995): S63–S74.

Williams, S. R., *Essentials of Nutrition and Diet Therapy*. 7th ed. St. Louis, Mo.: Mosby Press, 1999.

## Bulking Up/Slimming Down

Brownell, K. D., Steen, S. N., and Wilmore, J. H. "Weight Regulation Practices in Athletes: Analysis of Metabolic and Health Effects." *Medicine and Science in Sports and Exercise* 19 (1987): 546–556.

Constantini, N. W. "Clinical Consequences of Athletic Amenorrhea." *Sports Medicine* 17 (1994): 213–223.

## Building Muscle Mass and Strength

### ANABOLIC STEROIDS

Bhasin, S., Storer, T. W., Berman, N., Callegari, C., Clevenger, B., Phillips, J., Bunnell, T. J., Tricker, R., Shirazi, A. and Casburi, R. "The Effects of Supraphysiologic Doses of Testosterone on Muscle Size and Strength in Normal Men." *New England Journal of Medicine* 335 (1996): 1–7.

Franke, W. W. and Berendonk, B. "Hormonal Doping and Androgenization of Athletes: A Secret Program of the German Democratic Republic Government." *Clinical Chemistry* 43 (1997): 1262–1279.

Kadi, F., Eriksson, A., Holmner, S., and Thornell, L. E. "Effects of Anabolic Steroids on the Muscle Cells of Strength-trained Athletes." *Medicine and Sciences in Sports and Exercise* 31 (1999): 1528–1536.

Kadi, F. "Adaptation of Human Skeletal Muscle to Training and Anabolic Steroids." *Acta Physiologica Scandinavica, Supplementum* 646 (2000): 4–53.

King, D. S., Sharp, R. L., Vukovich, M. D., Brown, G. A., Reifenrath, T. A., Uhl, N. L., and Parsons, K. A. "Effect of Oral Androstenedione on Serum Testosterone and Adaptations to Resistance Training in Young Men: A Randomized Controlled Trial." *Journal of the American Medical Association* 281 (1999): 2020–2028.

Morales, A. J., Haubrich, R. H., Hwang, J. Y., Asakura, H., and Yen, S. S. C. "The Effect of Six Months Treatment with a 100 mg Daily Dose of Dehydroepiandrosterone (DHEA) on Circulating Sex Steroids, Body Composition and Muscle Strength in Age-Advanced Men and Women." *Clinical Endocrinology* 49 (1998): 421–432.

Pranav, K., and Henderson, S. "Priapism after Androstenedione Intake for Athletic Performance Enhancement." *Annals of Emergency Medicine* 35 (2000): 391–393.

Rasmussen, B. B., Volpi, E., Gore, D. C., and Wolfe, R. R. "Androstenedione Does Not Stimulate Muscle Protein Anabolism in Young Healthy Men." *Journal of Clinical Endocrinology and Metabolism* 85 (2000): 55–59.

Sullivan, M. L., Martinez, C. M., Gennis, M. P., and Gallagher, E. J. "The Cardiac Toxicity of Anabolic Steroids." *Progress in Cardiovascular Diseases* 41 (1998): 1–15.

Su, T. P., Pagliaro, M., Schmidt, P. J., Pickar, D., Wolkowitz, O., and Rubinow, W. R. "Neuropscyhiatric Effects of Anabolic Steroids in Male Normal Volunteers." *Journal of the American Medical Association* 269 (1993): 2760–2764.

Wilson, J. D. "Androgen Abuse by Athletes." *Endocrine Reviews* 9 (1988): 181–199.

## GROWTH HORMONE

Jenkins, P. J. "Growth Hormone and Exercise." *Clinical Endocrinology* 50 (1999): 683–689.

Karila, T., Koistinene, H., Seppala, M., Koistinen, R., and Seppala, T. "Growth Hormone Induced Increase in Serum IGFBP-3 Level Is Reserved by Anabolic Steroids in Substance Abusing Power Athletes." *Clinical Endocrinology* 49 (1998): 459–463.

Papadakis, M. A., Grady, D., Black, D., Tierney, M. J., Gooding, G. A. W., Schambelan, M., and Grunfeld, C. "Growth Hormone Replacement in Healthy Older Men Improves Body Composition But Not Functional Ability." *Annals of Internal Medicine* 124 (1996): 708–716.

Yarasheski, K. E., Zachwieja, J. J., Angelopoulos, T. J., and Bier, D. M. "Short-Term Growth Hormone Treatment Does Not Increase Muscle Protein Synthesis in Experienced Weight Lifters." *Journal of Applied Physiology* 74 (1993): 3073–3076.

## CREATINE PHOSPHATE

Bermon, S., Venembre, P., Sachet, C., Valour, S., and Dolisi, C. "Effects of Creatine Monohydrate Ingestion in Sedentary and Weight-trained Older Adults." *Acta Physiologica Scandinavica* 164 (1998): 147–155.

Bosco, C., Tihanyi, O. J., Pucspk, J., Kovacs, I., Gabossy, A., Colli, R., Pulvirenti, G., Tranquilli, C., Foti, C., Viru, M., Viru, A., Maganaris, C. N., and Maughan, R. J. "Creatine Supplementation Enhances Maximum Voluntary Isometric Force and Endurance Capacity in Resistance Trained Men." *Acta Physiologica Scandinavica* 163 (1998): 279–287.

Casey, A., Constatin-Teodosiu, D., Howell, S., Hultamn, E., and Greenhaf, P. L. "Creatine Ingestion Favorably Affects Performance and Muscle Metabolism during Maximal Exercise in Humans." *American Journal of Physiology* 271 (1996): E31–E37.

Englehardt, M., Neumann, G., Berbalk, A., and Reuter, I. "Creatine Supplementation in Endurance Sports." *Medicine and Science in Sports and Exercise* 30 (1998): 1123–1129.

Grindstaff, P. D., Kreider, R., Bishop, R., Wilson, M., Wood, L., Alexander, C., and Almada, "Effects of Creatine Supplementation on Repetitive Spring Performance and Body Composition in Competitive Swimmers." A. *International Journal of Sports Nutrition* 7 (1997): 330–346.

Kreider, R. B., Ferreira, M., Wilson, M., Grindstaff, P. Plisk, S., Reinardy, J., Cantlker, E., and Almada, A. L. "Effects of Creatine Supplementation on Body Composition, Strength and Spring Performance." *Medicine and Science in Sports and Exercise* 30 (1998): 73–82.

Maganari, C. N., and Maughan, R. J. "Creatine Supplementation Enhanced Maximum Voluntary Isometric Force and Endurance Capacity in Resistance Trained Men." *Acta Physiologica Scandinavica* 163 (1998): 279–287.

Mujika, I., Padilla, S., Ibanez, J., Izquierdo, M., and Gorostiaga, E. "Creatine Supplementation and Spring Performance in Soccer Players." *Medicine and Science in Sports and Exercise* 32 (2000): 518–525.

Peyrebrune, M. C., Nevill, M. E., Donaldson, F. J., and Cosford, D. J. "The Effects of Oral Creatine Supplementation on Performance in Single and Repeated Spring Swimming." *Journal of Sports Sciences* 16 (1998): 271–279.

Rawson, E. S., and Clarkson, P. M. "Acute Creatine Supplementation in Older Men." *International Journal of Sports Medicine* 20 (1999): 71–75.

Ro-Sanz, J., and Mendez-Marco, M. T. "Creatine Enhances Oxygen Uptake and Performance during Alternating Intensity Exercise." *Medicine and Science in Sports and Exercise* 32 (2000): 379–385.

Rossiter, H. B., Cannell, E. R., and Jakeman, P. M. "The Effect of Oral Creatine Supplementation on the 1000m Performance of Competitive Rowers." *Journal of Sports Sciences* 14 (1996): 175–179.

Snow, R. J., McKenna, M. J., Selig, S. E., Kemp, J., Stathis, C. G., and Zhao, S. "Effect of Creatine Supplementation on Sprint Exercise Performance and Muscle Metabolism." *Journal of Applied Physiology* 84 (1998): 1667–673.

Special Communication: American College of Sports Medicine. "Physiological and Health Effects of Oral Creatine Supplements." *Medicine and Science in Sports and Exercise* 32 (2000): 706–717.

Tihanyi, V. J., Kovacs, I., Gabossy, A., Colli, R., Pulvirentic, G., Tranquilli, C., Foti, C., Viru, M., and Viru, A. "Effect of Oral Creatine Supplementation on Jumping and Running Performance." *Journal of Sports Medicine* 18 (1997): 369–372.

Vandenberghe, K., Goris, M., Van Hecke, P., Van Leemputte, M., Vangerven, L., and Hespel, P. "Long-term Creatine Intake Is Beneficial to Muscle Performance during Resistance Training." *Journal of Applied Physiology* 83 (1997): 2055–2063.

Volek, J. S., Kraemer, W. J., Bush, J. A., Boetes, M., Incledon, T., Clark, K. L., and Lynch, J. M. "Creatine Supplementation Enhances Muscular Performance during High-Intensity Resistance Exercise." *Journal of the American Dietetic Association* 97 (1997): 765–770.

Williams, M. H. and Branch, J. D. "Creatine Supplementation and Exercise Performance: An Update." *Journal of the American College of Nutrition* 17 (1998): 216–234.

## OTHERS

Anderson, R. A. "Nutritional Factors Influencing the Glucose/Insulin System: Chromium." *Journal of the American College of Nutrition* 5 (1997): 404–410.

Clancy, S. P., Clarkson, P. M., DeCheke, M. E., Nosaka, K., Freedson, P. S., Cunninghman, J. J., and Valentine, B. "Effects of Chromium Picolinate Supplementation on Body Composition, Strength and Urinary Chromium Loss in Football Players." *International Journal of Sport Nutrition* 4 (1994): 142–153.

DiLuigi, L., Guidetti, L., Pigozzi, F., Baldari, C., Casini, A., Nordio, M., and Romanelli, F. "Acute Amino Acids Supplementation Enhances Pituitary Responsiveness in Athletes." *Medicine and Sciences in Sports and Exercise* 31 (1999): 1748–1759.

Kreider, R. B. "Dietary Supplements and the Promotion of Muscle Growth with Resistance Exercise." *Sports Medicine* 27 (1999): 97–110.

Mero, A. "Leucine Supplementation and Intensive Training." *Sports Medicine* 276 (1999): 347–358.

Nissen, S., Sharp, R., Ray, M., Rathmacher, J. A., Rice, D., Fuller, J. C., Connelly, A. S., and Abumrad, N. "Effect of Leucine Metabolite Beta-hydroxy-methylbutyrate on Muscle Metabolism during Resistance Exercise Training." *Journal of Applied Physiology* 81 (1996): 2095–2104.

Stanko, R. T., Robertson, R. J., Spina, R. J., Reilly, J. J., Greenawalt, K. D., and Goss, F. L. "Enhancement of Arm Exercise Endurance Capacity with Dihydroxyacetone and Pyruvate." *Journal of Applied Physiology* 68 (1990): 119–124.

Sukala, W. R. "Pyruvate: Beyond the Marketing Hype." *International Journal of Sports Nutrition* 8 (1998): 241–249.

# Getting Pumped

Adamson, J., and Vapnek, D. "Recombinant Erythropoietin to Improve Athletic Performance." *New England Journal of Medicine* 324 (1991): 698–699.

Bell, D. G., and Jacobs, I. "Combined Caffeine and Ephedrine Ingestion Improves Run Times of Canadian Forces Warrior Test." *Aviation Space Environmental Medicine* 70 (1999): 325–329.

Graham, T. E., and Spriet, L. L. "Metabolic, Catecholamine and Exercise Performance Responses to Various Doses of Caffeine." *Journal of Applied Physiology* 78 (1995): 867–874.

Graham, T. E. and Spriet, L. L. "Performance and Metabolic Responses to a High Caffeine Dose During Prolonged Exercise." *Journal of Applied Physiology* 71 (1991): 2292–2298.

Scott, W. "The Abuse of Erythropoietin to Enhance Athletic Performance." *Journal of the American Medical Association* 264 (1990): 1660–1990

Snell, P. "rHuEPO: Sport's Newest Drug Threat." *Orthopaedic Review* 21 (1992): 113–114.

Swain, R. A., Harsha, D. M., Baenziger, J., and Saywell, R. M. "Do Pseudoephedrine or Phenylpropanolamine Improve Maximum Oxygen Uptake and Time to Exhaustion?" *Clinical Journal of Sports Medicine* 7 (1997): 168–173.

Vahedi, K., Domigo, V., Amarenco, P., and Bousser, M. G. "Ischaemic Stroke in a Sportsman Who Consumed MaHuang Extract and Creatine Monohydrate for Body Building." *Journal of Neurology Neurosurgery and Psychiatry* 68 (2000): 112–113.

Vanakoski, J., Kosunen, V., Meririnne, E., and Seppala, T. "Creatine and Caffeine in Anaerobic and Aerobic Exercise: Effects on Physical Performance and Pharmacokinetic Considerations." *International Journal of Clinical Pharmacology and Therapeutics* 36 (1998): 258–263.

Vandenberghe, K., Gillis, N., Van Leemputte, M., Van Hecke, P., Vanstapel, F., and Hespel, P. "Caffeine Counteracts the Ergogenic Action of Muscle Creatine Loading." *Journal of Applied Physiology* 80 (1996): 452–457.

Zahn, K. A., Li, R. L., and Pursell, R. A. "Cardiovascular Toxicity after Ingestion of Herbal Ecstacy." *Journal of Emergency Medicine* 17 (1999): 289–291.

## Chilling Out

### ALCOHOL

Acheson, S., Stein, R., and Swartzwelder, H. S. Impairment of Semantic and Figural Memory by Acute Ethanol: Age-dependent Effects." *Alcoholism: Clinical and Experimental Research* 22 (7) (1998): 1437–1442.

Graham, T., and Dalton, J. "Effect of Alcohol on Man's Response to Mild Physical Activity in a Cold Environment." *Aviation, Space, and Environmental Medicine* 51 (1980): 793–796.

Little, P. J., Kuhn, C. M., Wilson, W. A., and Swartzwelder, H. S. "Differential Effects of Ethanol in Adolescent and Adult Rats." *Alcoholism: Clinical and Experimental Research* 20 (8) (1996): 1346–1351.

Markweise, B., Acheson, S., Levin, E., Wilson, W., and Swartzwelder, H. S. "Differential Effects of Ethanol on Memory in Adolescent and Adult Rats." *Alcoholism: Clinical and Experimental Research* 22 (2) (1998): 416–421.

Markiewicz, K., and Cholewa, M. "The Effect of Alcohol on the Circulatory System Adaptation to Physical Effort." *Journal of Studies on Alcohol* 43 (1982): 812–823.

McNaughton, L., and Preece, D. "Alcohol and Its Effects on Middle Distance Running." *British Journal of Sports Medicine* 20 (1986): 56–59.

Pyapali, G., Turner, D., Wilson, W., and Swartzwelder, H. S. "Age and Dose-Dependent Effects of Ethanol on the Induction of Hippocampal Long-Term Potentiation." *Alcohol* 19 (2) (1999): 107–111.

Swartzwelder, H. S., Wilson, W. A., and Tayyeb, M. I. "Differential Sensitivity of NMDA Receptor-Mediated Synaptic Potentials to Ethanol in Immature vs. Mature Hippocampus." *Alcoholism: Clinical and Experimental Research* 19 (1995): 320–323.

Swartzwelder, H. S., Richardson, R., Markwiese, B., Wilson, W., and Little, P. "Developmental Differences in the Acquisition of Tolerance to Ethanol." *Alcohol* 15 (4) (1998): 311–314.

### MARIJUANA

Bird, K., Boleyn, T., Chesher, G., Jackson, D., Starmer, G., and Teo, R. "Intercannabinoid and Cannabinoid-Ethanol Interactions and Their Effects on Human Performance." *Psychopharmacology* 71 (1980): 181–188.

Duncan, D. "Reasons for Discontinuing Hashish Use in a Group of Central European Athletes." *Journal of Drug Education* 18 (1988): 49–53.

Renaud, A., and Cormier, Y. "Acute Effects of Marihuana Smoking on Maximal Exercise Performance." *Medicine and Science in Sports and Exercise* 18 (1986): 685–689.

Wu, T., Tashkin, D., Djahed, B., and Rose, J. "Pulmonary Hazards of Smoking Marijuana as Compared with Tobacco." *New England Journal of Medicine* 318 (1988): 347–351.

## Smoking and Chewing

Edwards, S., Glover, E., and Schroeder, K. "The Effects of Smokeless Tobacco on Heart Rate and Neuromuscular Reactivity in Athletes and Nonathletes." *The Physician and Sports Medicine* 15 (1987): 141–147.

Landers, D., Crews, D., Boutcher, S., Skinner, J., and Gustafsen, S. "The Effects of Smokeless Tobacco on Performance and Psychophysiological Response." *Medicine and Science in Sports and Exercise* 24 (1992): 895–903.

Van Duser, B., and Raven, P. "The Effects of Oral Smokeless Tobacco on the Cardiorespiratory Response to Exercise." *Medicine and Science in Sports and Exercise* 24 (1992): 389–395.

# INDEX

acetaminophen, 166
acetylcholine, 20
acromegaly, 87
addiction, 46–48
  compulsion vs., 48
  reward system and, 47–48, 79–80,
    152
  tolerance and, 44–45, 47–48, 152
  *see also specific drugs*
adenosine triphosphate (ATP), 29, 91
  body's creation of, 21–22
  caffeine and, 62, 124
  fatigue and, 25
adolescents:
  alcohol use by, 72, 138–39, 149
  marijuana use by, 72, 148
  nicotine use by, 72, 156, 157
  steroid use by, 14, 71–72, 74–75
adrenal glands, 84, 106
aerobic metabolism, sustained exercise
    and, 21, 25, 28, 29, 93
aging:
  DHEA levels and, 84–85
  growth hormone and, 86
albuterol:

as asthma drug, 19, 42, 104
  delivery method of, 42
alcohol, 131–42
  acute effects of, 132–39, 149
  addiction to, 47, 113, 139–42
  biphasic effects of, 132, 137
  brain and, 46, 134–36, 138
  chronic effects of, 139–42, 149
  coordination impaired by, 132, 135,
    139, 142
  effects on adults vs. adolescents,
    138–39, 149
  exercise and, 131–42
  kava kava and, 163
  sedatives combined with, 162
alertness, ephedrine and, 115
alpha-methyldopa, 89
alpha receptors, 107, 109, 110, 120
alprazolam (Xanax), 161
Alzedo, Lyle, 76
Ambien (zolpidem), 162
amenorrhea, 63, 74, 166, 168
American College of Sports Medicine,
    72
amino acids, 22, 24

complementary, 97
  as energy source, 96
  as growth-hormone releasing agents,
    89
  insulin and, 94
  proteins broken down into, 96
  sources of, 96–97
  types of, 100–101
amino acid supplements, 24, 34, 95–96
  cost of, 99
amphetamine, 108, 109, 110, 118
  action of, 114
  addiction to, 47, 58, 104, 113
  athletic performance and, 46, 114–15
  delivery method for, 115
  development of, 104–5, 113
  risks of, 109, 114, 115–16
  uses for, 104–5, 114
anabolic steroids, 14, 32, 38, 68–83
  absorbed through skin, 43
  action of, 68–69, 72–73
  addiction and, 48, 79–80
  body's storage of, 44
  dangers of, 37, 70, 73–80, 81, 86, 101
  delivery methods for, 80, 81, 82
  dose regimens of, 37, 72–73, 81, 83
  hypomania and, 78–79, 80
  lists of, 82–83
  "natural and safe," 84–85
  Olympic athletes' use of, 70–71
  preparations of, 80–81
  psychological effects of, 77–79
  tolerance and, 45
anaerobic metabolism, short-term exer-
    cise and, 21, 25, 27, 29
androstenedione (andro), 75, 84
anesthetics, 46, 89, 112, 113, 164
animal studies, validity of, 33, 34
anorexia nervosa, 58
antibiotics, 40
antidepressants, 169–70
  appropriate use of, 170
anxiety disorders, 161, 162
  see also performance anxiety
appetite suppressants, 56–58, 114
  action of, 56, 57
  effectiveness of, 56, 65
  marketing of, 56–57
  risks of, 57, 58
arginine, 89, 100

aspirin, 33, 166, 167
asthma, 40, 104, 105
  athletic performance and, 19, 119,
    120
  drug treatment for, 19, 42, 107, 110,
    119–20
atenolol, 169
athletes:
  body weight concerns of, 51–65
  endurance, see endurance athletes
  goals of, 31–32
  rewards for, 13, 16
  superstitious rituals of, 48
athletes, female:
  amenorrhea in, 63, 74, 166, 168
  daily protein requirements for, 98
  smokeless tobacco use by, 155
  steroids and, 38, 70–71, 74
  weight-loss issues and, 63
athletes, male:
  daily protein requirements for, 98
  smokeless tobacco use by, 153, 155
  steroid dosages of, 37, 72–73, 81, 83
ATP, see adenosine triphosphate
attention deficit hyperactivity disorder
    (ADHD), medication for, 110,
    118–19
autonomic nervous system:
  exercise and, 17–18, 19, 26–27, 28,
    29
  stimulants and, 17

barbiturates, 161–62
basal ganglia, 145
basal metabolism, 51, 53
  body weight and, 52
  in men vs. women, 52
beta blockers, 168–69
  hazards of, 169
beta receptors, 90, 107, 109, 110
  blocking of, 168–69
birth control pills, 40
  for estrogen replacement, 63
blood, oxygenation of, 18, 19, 125–27
blood doping, 125–28
blood glucose, 17, 22, 29, 42, 87, 94, 107
blood pressure:
  appetite suppressants and, 57
  decongestants and, 121
  diuretics and, 54

ephedrine and, 64
thyroid hormone and, 60
body temperature:
  alcohol's effects on, 136–37
  amphetamine and, 114
  exercise and, 19
body weight:
  basal metabolism and, 52
  formula for, 51–52
  gaining and losing of, 50–65
brain:
  alcohol's acute effects on, 46, 134–36,
    138
  appetite suppressants and, 57
  brawn vs., 18
  chronic drinking and, 141–42
  drug addiction and, 47–48, 49, 79–80
  exercise and, 17–18, 19, 26–27, 28
  hunger and satiety centers of, 56
  lactic acid and, 26
  marijuana's acute effects on, 144–46
  nicotine and, 151–52
  reward system in, 47–48, 79–80, 113,
    152
  stimulants and, 109, 110, 112, 113,
    114
  training-induced changes in, 26–27,
    29
  *see also* autonomic nervous system;
    sympathetic nervous system
"branched chain" amino acids, 100
brawn, brain vs., 18
breast tissue, steroids and, 75, 80, 82, 84
bronchioles, 122
  in asthma, 19, 91, 116, 119
  sympathetic nervous system and, 107
bronchitis, chronic, 143
bronchodilators, oral vs. inhaled,
    119–20
brown fat, 61
bulimia nervosa, 58
Butler, Brett, 157

caffeine, 45, 104, 105, 109
  action of, 122, 123–24
  athletic performance and, 122, 123,
    128
  creatine combined with, 93
  dangers of, 124
  ephedrine combined with, 64, 65, 123

long-term use of, 124–25
  safety of, 12
  in weight-loss drugs, 33, 61–62, 64,
    122, 124
  withdrawal from, 123
calcium, 124
calcium supplements, 41
calories, burning of, 52, 53
cancer:
  smokeless tobacco and, 156, 157
  smoking and, 143, 156, 157
  steroids and, 76, 80
  *see also specific cancers*
carbohydrate loading, 23
carbohydrates, energy from, 21, 22–23,
    99, 101
carbon monoxide, 158
carcinogens, in tobacco vs. marijuana,
    143
cardiomyopathy, 116
cardiovascular system:
  blood doping and, 127
  during exercise, 17, 19, 26, 27, 29
  steroids and, 70, 73, 74, 75–76, 80
  stimulants and, 110–11, 115, 117–18,
    120, 121, 124, 127, 128
  training and, 26, 27, 28, 29
Carpenter, Karen, 59
cartilage, 73, 80, 86
catabolic steroids, asthma treated by, 69
cerebellum, 142, 145
chewing tobacco, *see* smokeless tobacco
cholesterol:
  estrogen and, 63, 76
  HDL, 76, 140, 149
  LDL, 76
  steroids and, 76, 80
chromium piccolinate, 95, 101
cigars, 151, 152
circulatory system, *see* cardiovascular
    system
clenbuterol, 68
  asthma and, 91
  in food animals, 90
clonidine, 89
cocaine, 104, 109, 111–13
  action of, 112, 113
  addictiveness of, 47, 79, 111, 112–13
  as anesthetic, 112, 113
  athletic performance and, 111, 112–13

cocaine (*continued*)
  autonomic nervous system and, 17
  delivery of, 112
coca leaves, 104, 111
codeine, 165
compulsion, addiction vs., 48
coordination, 132, 135, 139, 142, 145,
    146, 161, 162
cortisol, 68–69, 85
  as asthma treatment, 69
  excess testosterone and, 73
creatine phosphate, 43, 91–93
  caffeine combined with, 93
  as energy source, 24–25, 29, 91, 92,
    101
  training and, 28, 32, 93
Creutzfeldt-Jakob disease, 86, 87
cross-training:
  cardiovascular changes and, 28
  limitations of, 27
cycling, cyclists, 20, 21, 25, 27, 124

dancing, calories burned by, 53
decongestants, 46, 104, 110
  action of, 120–21
  risks of, 121
dehydration:
  diuretic use and, 55
  kidneys and, 54
  purging and, 59
delta-9-tetrahydrocannabinol (THC), *see*
    THC
Demerol (meperidine), 165
dental cavities, smokeless tobacco and,
    157
depression, treatment of, 169–70
diabetes, 87, 94
diarrhea, 63
diazepam (Valium), 161, 162, 166
diet, protein in, 98
dieting:
  double-edged sword of, 52, 65
  energy consumption and, 53
dihydroepiandrosterone (DHEA),
    84–85
dinitrophenol (DNP):
  action of, 60–61, 65
  dangers of, 60–61, 65
diuretics, 53–55, 124
  banned by sports federations, 55

blood pressure lowered by, 54
kidneys and, 54
side effects of, 55, 65
dopamine, 57, 116
  amphetamine and, 114
  cocaine and, 112–13
driving:
  alcohol and, 135, 139
  marijuana and, 146
Drug Enforcement Agency (DEA), 79
drugs, 39–49
  action of, 41–44
  body's elimination of, 41, 44, 80, 81
  cell receptors for, 41–42, 48–49
  definition of, 40
  delivery methods for, 42–43
  purposes of, 40
  societal acceptance of, 16
  tolerance and, *see* tolerance, drug
drugs, recreational, 14, 129–49
  *see also* cocaine; heroin; marijuana
drugs and supplements, performance-
    enhancing, 40–41
  acceptable, 38
  effervescent preparations of, 43
  evaluating claims of, 33–38
  evidence for claims of, 35
  illegal use of, 32, 44, 55, 71, 72, 84,
    85, 109–10, 117, 119–20, 126,
    127, 165, 169, 170
  long-term safety of, 37–38
  motives for taking, 13–14, 16, 32,
    70–71
  training benefits reduced by, 28, 32,
    93, 108, 158–59, 165–66
  weight loss and, *see* weight-loss drugs
    and supplements
  *see also specific drugs and supplements*

eating:
  brain signals for, 56
  exercise after, 19
effervescent preparations, 43
electrolytes, loss of, 58
Eli Lilly, 104–5, 113
endorphins:
  amenorrhea and, 168
  "runner's high" and, 167–68
endurance:
  marijuana and, 144

nicotine and, 155
endurance athletes:
aerobic metabolism and, 21, 25, 28, 29, 93
blood doping by, 125–27
carbohydrate loading by, 23
slow-twitch muscle fibers of, 20, 27
training by, 27–28
energy:
from food, 21–24, 25, 29, 96–99, 101
lifestyle and, 53
for muscle movement, 21, 24–25, 27, 28, 29, 95–101
enkephalins, 167
ephedrine, 109, 116–18
action of, 116
alertness and, 115
asthma and, 40, 104–5, 113, 116, 122
athletic performance and, 116–18
autonomic nervous system and, 17
caffeine combined with, 64, 65
dangers of, 64, 117–18
signs of excessive use of, 118
sympathetic nervous system and, 61, 64, 116
weight loss and, 33, 40, 58, 61, 64, 116
epinephrine (adrenaline):
action of, 106–7
beta blockers and, 168–69
erectile dysfunction, smoking and, 159
erythropoietin (EPO), blood doping and, 126–27
esophagus, damaged by vomiting, 58
estradiol, 80, 82
androstenedione converted to, 75, 84
estrogen, 63, 76
ethanol, 161
exercise:
alcohol and, 131–42
antidepressants and, 169–70
brain's role in, 17–18, 19, 26–27, 28, 29
cardiovascular system and, 17, 19, 26, 27, 29
eating before, 19
energy use increased through, 53
lifestyle and, 53
lungs and, 17, 18–19, 26, 27, 28, 29
marijuana and, 142–49

muscles and, 20–21, 24–25, 27–28, 29
nicotine and, 151–59
sedatives and, 161–70
stimulants and, 58, 102–28
sympathetic nervous system and, 105–9
weight loss and, 52–53, 65
eyes, sympathetic nervous system and, 107

facial features, enlargement of, 87
FACTREL (gonadotropin releasing hormone; gonadorelin), 83
fast-twitch muscle fibers, sprinting and, 20, 27
"fat-blocking" drugs, 62–63
"fat-burning" drugs, 24, 59–62
danger of, 59
*see also* thyroid hormone; *specific drugs*
fatigue:
ATP and, 25
lactic acid buildup and, 26, 29
"fat-melting" creams, 62
fats:
brown, 61
caffeine and, 33, 61–62, 64, 122, 124
energy from, 18, 21, 22, 23–24, 25, 29
insulin injections and, 94
percentage of body weight in, 23
fat-soluble vitamins, 63
fatty acids, 22, 23
fenfluramine, 57–58
fen-phen, 57
fentanyl, 165
fidgeting, weight loss and, 52
flatulence, 63
Fleischl-Marxow, Ernst von, 111
"flight or fight" response, 105, 109
fluoxetine (Prozac), 169
Food and Drug Administration (FDA), 60
Freud, Sigmund, 111
furosemide, 55

gamma-butyrolactone (GBL), 163–64
gamma hydroxybutyrate (GHB):
ineffectiveness of, 88, 164
marketing of, 164
overdoses of, 88, 89, 163–64
glucagon, 105, 107

glucose, blood, 17, 22, 29, 42, 87, 94, 107
glutamine, 100
glycogen, 96
    carbohydrate loading and, 23
    storage of, 22, 23–24, 29
gonadotropin releasing hormone
        (gonadorelin; FACTREL), 83
growth hormone, 43, 85–90, 101
    action of, 86
    alcohol's interference with, 135–36
    forms of, 87
    side effects of, 87
growth-hormone releasing agents,
        88–89
Gugliota, Tom, 164
gum recession, 157

Halcion (triazolam), 162
hCG (human chorionic gonadotropin),
        81, 83
heart:
    alcohol's acute effects on, 133, 149
    alcohol's chronic effects on, 140–41
    alcohol's positive effect on, 140, 149
    amphetamine damage to, 116
    autonomic nervous system and, 17, 19
    decongestants and, 121
    ephedrine and, 117, 118
    ipecac and, 59
    marijuana and, 144, 149
    smokeless tobacco and, 154–55
    smoking and, 158–59
    steroid damage to, 73, 75–76
    sympathetic nervous system and, 107
    see also cardiovascular system
heart attacks:
    ephedrine and, 64
    estrogen deficiency and, 63
height, steroids and, 74
"Herban Ecstasy," see ephedrine
heredity:
    alcohol and, 132
    energy consumption determined by,
        53
    heart size and, 19
    lung volume and, 18–19
    muscle performance and, 20
heroin, 165
    addiction to, 47, 79, 113

high-density lipoproteins (HDLs):
    alcohol and, 140, 149
    steroids and, 76
hippocampus, 135, 141, 145
histamine, 120, 121
HIV, transmission of, 87
horses, diuretics and, 54
human chorionic gonadotropin (hCG),
        81, 83
hunger center, of brain, 56
hypomania, steroids and, 78–79, 80
hypothermia, 137

ibuprofen, 166, 167
IGF (somatomedin), 88
impotence, 36, 73
improvement:
    evaluating claims for, 33–37
    personal definition of, 31–32
infertility, 36
inhalers, 42, 119
inhaling, of drugs, 42, 112, 114, 119,
        120, 121
injections, of drugs, 42, 43–44, 82
insomnia, 64
insulin, 42, 94, 105, 107
    chromium piccolinate and, 95
International Olympic Committee
        (IOC), substances banned by,
        109–10
interval training, 25
ipecac, 58–59
Iron Man triathlon, 25
isoleucine, 100

jockeys, diuretic use by, 54
Jurassic Park, 97

kava kava, 163
kidneys, 126
    diuretics and, 54
    drug elimination and, 44

lactic acid, fatigue and, 26, 29
laxatives, 58, 59
learning:
    alcohol and, 134–35, 138, 141–42
    marijuana and, 145–46, 149
leucine, 100

leukoplakia, smokeless tobacco and, 157
libido, steroids and, 74, 75, 80
lifestyle, exercise and, 53
ligaments, steroids and, 73, 80
liver:
    autonomic nervous system and, 17
    drug elimination and, 44, 80, 81
    glucose released by, 17, 22, 29
    growth hormone and, 86, 87
    steroids and, 77, 80, 82
    sympathetic nervous system and, 107
low-density lipoproteins (LDLs), 76
lung cancer:
    marijuana and, 143
    smoking and, 158
lungs:
    alcohol and, 134, 141
    autonomic nervous system and, 17
    in drug inhalation, 42
    exercise and, 17, 18–19, 26, 27, 28, 29
    smoking and, 142–44, 149, 158–59
    volume of, 18–19
luteinizing hormone, 43–44, 83
lysine, 89

McGwire, Mark, 84
Ma Huang, *see* ephedrine
marijuana, 142–49
    acute effects of, 144–46
    adolescent use of, 72, 148
    chronic effects of, 146–48, 149
    coordination impaired by, 145, 146
    smoking of, 142–44, 149
memory:
    alcohol and, 135, 138, 141–42
    marijuana and, 145–46, 147–48, 149
menstrual cycles, disruption of, 37, 63,
        74, 166, 168
meperidine (Demerol), 165
Meridia (sibutramine), 57–58
methamphetamine, 118
methylphenidate (Ritalin), 118–19
mitochondria, training and, 27
morphine, 165
mouth, diseases of, 156–57
mucous membranes, drug entry
        through, 42, 153
muscle fibers:
    training and, 20–21, 27

types of, 20, 27
muscle mass:
    amino acids and, 96–101
    clenbuterol and, 90–91
    energy consumption determined by,
        52, 53
    of men vs. women, 69
    steroids and, 45, 68–83
muscle recovery:
    alcohol as disruptive to, 136
    amino acids and, 100–101
muscles:
    action of, 19–20
    brain and, 17–18, 26–27
    chronic drinking and, 140–41, 149
    composition of, 19–20
    energy sources for, 17, 18, 21–25,
        27–28, 29, 95–101
    energy stores in, 21, 24–25, 43,
        91–93
    exercise and, 20–21, 24–25, 27–28, 29
    fatigue, 25–26
    sympathetic nervous system and, 107
    training and, 20–21, 27–28, 29

naloxone (Narcan), 168
nandrolone, 44
narcolepsy, 89, 164
narcotic analgesics, 164–67
    action of, 165, 166, 167
    addiction to, 166
    dangers of, 166
    purpose of, 165, 170
nasal decongestants, 120–21, 110
nasal surgery, cocaine used in, 112, 113
National Institute of Drug Abuse
        (NIDA), 79
nerves:
    as movement initiators, 20
    training and, 26
nervous system, *see* autonomic nervous
        system; sympathetic nervous
        system
neurotransmitters:
    amino acids as building blocks for, 96
    stimulated by appetite suppressants,
        57
    of sympathetic nervous system, *see*
        epinephrine; norepinephrine

nicotine, 42, 151–59
　action of, 151–52
　addiction to, 47, 113, 151–52
　adolescents' use of, 72, 156, 157
　exercise and, 151–59
　see also smokeless tobacco; smoking
nicotine gum, 152, 157–58
nicotine patches, 152, 157–58
nonsteroidal anti-inflammatory drugs,
　　166–67
norepinephrine (noradrenaline):
　action of, 105–8, 168–69
　amphetamine and, 114
　beta blockers and, 168–69
　cocaine's interaction with, 112
　ephedrine and, 116
　increased by stimulants, 109, 110–11
　weight-loss drugs and, 57, 61
Nutrition Facts Manual (Bloch, Shils,
　　Williams, and Wilkins), 98

obesity, drugs for, see weight-loss drugs
　　and supplements
Olympic Committee, U.S. (USOC),
　　substances banned by, 55, 84,
　　109–10
opiates, see narcotic analgesics
oral cancer, 156, 157
Orlistat, 62–63
　side effects of, 63
ornithine, 100
oxygen:
　in blood, 18, 19, 125–27
　energy production and, 21, 25, 26

pancreas, sympathetic nervous system
　　and, 107
panic disorder, 26
paroxetine (Paxil), 169
peliosis hepatitis, 77
pemoline, 110, 118–19
penicillin, 40
performance anxiety:
　alcohol and, 134–35
　beta blockers and, 168–69
periodontal disease, smokeless tobacco
　　and, 157
phentermine, 57
pills, drugs taken as, 42–44
pituitary gland, 85, 88

placebo effect, 48
platelets, steroids and, 76
polynuclear aromatic hydrocarbons, 143
potassium, 55, 58
pregnancy test, 83
primary pulmonary hypertension, 57
"prohormones," 85
propranolol, 89, 169
prostate cancer, steroids and, 76, 80
prostate gland, 121
proteins:
　best sources of, 96–97
　broken down into amino acids, 22, 96
　as energy source, 24, 95–101
　supplements, see amino acid supple-
　　ments
Prozac (fluoxetine), 169–70
pseudoephedrine, see decongestants
puberty:
　premature, 43
　testosterone and, 69, 70
purging, 58, 59, 65
pyramid regimens, steroids taken in, 81,
　　83

reaction time, smokeless tobacco and,
　　156
receptors, drug, 41–42, 46, 48–49, 73
recombinant DNA, blood doping and,
　　126
red blood cells, enhancing of, 125–27
reproductive system:
　steroids and, 75, 80
　testosterone and, 69, 70
reward system, in brain, 47–48, 79–80,
　　113, 152
Ritalin (methylphenidate), 118–19
Rohyphnol ("roofies"), 162
"roid rage," 77–79
"runner's high," 167–68
running, long-distance, 20, 21, 25, 27,
　　124, 167–68

satiety center, of brain, 56
sedatives, 161–70
　alcohol and, 162
　athletic performance and, 161, 162,
　　165–66, 168–69
　types of, see specific sedatives
seizures, 64, 113, 164

selective serotonin reuptake inhibitors
(SSRIs), 113, 169–70
selenium, toxicity of, 41
serotonin, 57
increased by cocaine, 113, 169
increased by SSRIs, 169–70
sertraline (Zoloft), 169
sibutramine (Meridia), 57–58
skin:
drugs absorbed through, 43
sympathetic nervous system and, 107
sleep:
alcohol and, 135–36
growth hormone produced in, 89–90
sedatives and, 162
slow-twitch muscle fibers, endurance
events and, 20, 27
slow-wave sleep, 90
smokeless tobacco, 151, 152, 153–57
athletes' use of, 153, 155
effects of smoking vs., 153–54
health risks of, 156–57, 159
types of, 42, 153
smoking:
effects of smokeless tobacco vs.,
153–54
erectile dysfunction and, 159
health risks of, 158–59
lungs and, 142–44, 149, 158–59
nicotine delivered through, 42, 152
sports and, 158–59
smoking cessation programs, 152, 157
snuff, 42, 153, 154
sodium, 54, 58
soft tissue lesions, smokeless tobacco
and, 157
somatomedin (IGF), 88
sperm, production of, 69
steroids and, 73, 75
spleen, 87
sports culture, smokeless tobacco and,
153, 155
sprinters:
energy for, 21, 25, 27, 29, 91, 92, 101
fast-twitch muscle fibers of, 20, 27
training-induced changes in, 27
SSRIs (selective serotonin reuptake
inhibitors), 113, 169–70
starch, 22
*Steroid Nightmare* (Vinchattle), 78

steroids:
anabolic, *see* anabolic steroids
catabolic, 69
veterinary, 82
stimulants, 90, 102–25
action of, 108–11, 127
addiction to, 47, 58, 109
autonomic nervous system and, 17
danger of, 32, 58, 110–11, 127
as "fat-burning" drugs, 61
quiz on, 104
risk/reward equation for, 108
risky dosages of, 109, 121, 122, 123
as sympathetic nervous system mim-
ics, 106
tolerance and, 45, 47, 125
training and, 108, 114, 115, 117, 118,
122, 125
*see also specific stimulants*
strokes, 64
studies, scientific:
on alcohol, 133, 136, 137, 138, 141
on androstenedione, 84
on appetite suppressants, 56
on amino acids, 34
on bronchodilators, 119
on caffeine consumption, 123
on chromium piccolinate, 95
on creatine phosphate, 92
on ephedrine, 117
evaluation of, 33–35, 37–38
on glutamine, 100
on marijuana, 143, 144, 146–48
on muscle fibers, 20–21
on smokeless tobacco, 154–55
on steroids, 71
on testosterone and aggression, 77–78
on thinness and fidgeting, 52
on weight loss, 33–35
sugars:
in American diet, 22
in ATP creation, 21
muscles powered by, 18
*see also* blood glucose
swimming, 21
sympathetic nervous system (SNS), 57,
60, 90
athletic performance and, 105–9
beta blockers and, 168–69
nicotine and, 151–52

sympathetic nervous system (SNS) (continued)
  stimulants and, 61, 64, 104–25

tar, 143
teeth, vomiting as damaging to, 58
tendons, steroids and, 73, 80, 86
tension, in muscles, 27
testicles, steroids and, 75, 81, 83
testicular cancer, steroids and, 76, 80
testicular powder, 85
testosterone, 32, 37, 44, 68
  cortisol receptors and, 73
  natural effects of, 69, 70, 76
  precursors of, 75, 84–85
  puberty and, 43, 69, 70
  Tribulus and, 36–37
  women athletes and, 38, 70–71
THC (delta-9-tetrahydrocannabinol),
    143
  long-lasting effects of, 146
  receptors in brain, 145
theophylline:
  asthma and, 122
  weight loss and, 61–62, 122
thinking, marijuana and, 147
thyroid gland, 59–60
thyroid hormone (triiodothyronine),
    59–60
  delivery method for, 43–44
  hazards of, 60, 65
tobacco, see smokeless tobacco; smoking
tolerance, drug, 44–45, 79–80, 125, 152
  adolescents and, 139
  causes of, 45, 47
training:
  alcohol and, 134, 136–37
  bodily functions changed by, 26–28,
    29, 32, 93, 108
  energy and, 53, 97–100
  goals of, 32
  marijuana and, 145–46
  muscle fibers and, 20–21, 27

narcotic analgesics and, 165–66
nicotine and, 154–55, 158–59
purpose of, 26
sedatives and, 161, 162, 165–66
stimulants and, 108, 114, 115, 117,
    118, 122, 125
  see also exercise
triazolam (Halcion), 162
Tribulus terrestris, 36–37

valine, 100
Valium (diazepam), 161, 162, 166
veterinary steroids, 82
Vinchattle, Kirk, 78
visual processing, marijuana and, 148,
    149
vitamins, fat-soluble, 63
vitamin supplements, effectiveness of,
    41
vomiting, 58–59, 65
Vonnegut, Kurt, 62

walking, 53
"water weight," loss of, 53–55
weight, body, see body weight
weight lifters, weight lifting, 21, 118
  GHB use by, 88
  pre-competition diets of, 99–100
  steroid use by, 45, 70, 71
weight loss, exercise and, 52–53, 65
weight-loss drugs and supplements, 40,
    50–65, 110, 116
  evaluating studies of, 33–35
  tolerance and, 45
  see also appetite suppressants; diuretics; "fat-burning" drugs; "fat-blocking" drugs; specific drugs and
    supplements
wrestlers, diuretic use by, 54

Xanax (alprazolam), 161

zolpidem (Ambien), 162